Remembering Oscar Romero and the Martyrs of El Salvador

Remembering Oscar Romero and the Martyrs of El Salvador

A Cloud of Witnesses

John S. Thiede, SJ

LEXINGTON BOOKS
Lanham • Boulder • New York • London

Published by Lexington Books
An imprint of The Rowman & Littlefield Publishing Group, Inc.
4501 Forbes Boulevard, Suite 200, Lanham, Maryland 20706
www.rowman.com

Unit A, Whitacre Mews, 26-34 Stannary Street, London SE11 4AB

Copyright © 2017 by Lexington Books

All rights reserved. No part of this book may be reproduced in any form or by any electronic or mechanical means, including information storage and retrieval systems, without written permission from the publisher, except by a reviewer who may quote passages in a review.

British Library Cataloguing in Publication Information Available

The hardback edition of this book was previously cataloged by the Library of Congress as follows:

Library of Congress Cataloging-in-Publication Data

Names: Thiede, John S. (John Spencer), author.
Title: Remembering Oscar Romero and the martyrs of El Salvador : a cloud of witnesses / John Thiede.
Description: Lanham : Lexington Books, 2017. | Includes bibliographical references and index.
Identifiers: LCCN 2017013135 (print) | LCCN 2017014078 (ebook)
Subjects: LCSH: Martyrdom—Christianity. | Catholic Church—Doctrines. | Persecution—El Salvador—History—20th century. | Romero, ?Oscar A. (?Oscar Arnulfo), 1917-1980. | El Salvador—Church history—20th century.
Classification: LCC BR1601.3 (ebook) | LCC BR1601.3 .T425 2017 (print) | DDC 272/.9097284—dc23
LC record available at https://lccn.loc.gov/2017013135

ISBN 978-1-4985-3798-8 (cloth)
ISBN 978-1-4985-3799-5 (electronic)
ISBN 978-1-4985-3800-8 (pbk.)

Contents

Acknowledgments		vii
Introduction		ix
1	The Definition of Martyrdom: Early Martyrdom to Middle Ages	1
2	Martyrdom in Contemporary Times	9
3	The Reality of Martyrdom in Latin America/El Salvador	25
4	Four Examplars: Rutilio Grande, Archbishop Romero, U.S. Churchwomen, UCA Martyrs	35
5	Martyrdom in *Christology at the Crossroads* (pre-1989)	67
6	Martyrdom in *Jesus the Liberator/Christ the Liberator* (post-1989)	83
Conclusion: The Reality of Martyrdom Today		103
Bibliography		111
Index		117
About the Author		125

Acknowledgments

I am incredibly grateful to the many people who supported me during the writing of this book, especially anyone I may have forgotten to thank personally. First and foremost I want to thank all of my Notre Dame faculty mentors for getting me started on this project. Thanks especially to Matt Ashley who, after directing my dissertation, has continued to serve as mentor and friend. Thank you to Larry Cunningham for the many conversations about theology and martyrdom. Thank you to Gustavo Gutiérrez, for opening up the larger panorama of Latin America, our many lunch conversations, and the unique insights and inspiration to always remember the preferential option for the poor. And thank you to the faculty of the Notre Dame theology department and especially the Systematic Theology faculty, who helped me find my vocation as a theologian. I also want to thank my friends from theology studies at Notre Dame, especially Peter Fritz who read through drafts of this project and provided the artwork for the cover. Thanks as well to Matt Eggemeier who read through drafts and encouraged me to continue researching and writing.

I am also thankful to the theology department and Jesuit community at Marquette University. Phil Rossi, SJ has served as my faculty mentor and generously read drafts of this project. Bob Doran, SJ provided encouragement as did many other faculty members at Marquette. Mike Guzik, SJ, Greg O'Meara, SJ, Craig Hightower, SJ, Bill Sheahan, SJ and the "young priest" group in Milwaukee supported me through friendship and prayers. Thanks as well to my research assistants Alexandre Martins and Sara Hulse. Marquette also gave me research leave to work on this project. Thanks to Boston College and the Jesuit community for the writing fellowship, especially university President Bill Leahy, SJ for his support, and Jim Keenan, SJ for his mentoring and help writing the proposal which would eventually lead to the book contract, and to the Roberts House Jesuit Community. Thanks to the Jesuit Community at Universidad Alberto Hurtado in Santiago, Chile for giving me access to the theology library to research and an office where I could write. Thanks especially to provincial Cristian Del Campo, SJ, rector Eduardo Silva, SJ, Jorge Costadoat, SJ, and Fernando Verdugo, SJ for their critique of my work.

I am incredibly grateful to all at Lexington Books for shepherding me through this process. Sarah Craig was very patient with me and provided excellent editorial support. While I received much guidance and advice from many which certainly improved this book, all errors or omissions are my own. Finally, I want to thank my extended family for their love and support during the writing of this book. I want to thank my brother Jeff Thiede, his wife Susan, and their three kids Ben, Parker, and Joe. Thank you to my sister Kay Paulus, her husband Mike, and their three kids Sean, Autumn, and Maureen. Thank you to my mom, Kathleen Thiede, for your continual encouragement and constant show of love. While my dad, Len Thiede, died five years ago after a battle with neuro-endocrine cancer when I was still finishing my PhD work, his zest for life, care and concern for others, and jovial spirit will always be an inspiration. I dedicate this book to my dad and his enduring love and legacy.

John Thiede, SJ

Introduction

With Pope John Paul II and his universal call to holiness more men and women were canonized than by any of his recent predecessors. He had no preference for continents nor numbers of miracles. John Paul II simply wanted to give a number of examples to inspire the faithful to live more holy lives. Perhaps not coincidentally this interest in the saints also increased interest in the martyrs. Scholars began to write about them and they also captured the imagination of the faithful. In fact, the story of the monks of Tiburine in Algeria even became the topic of a movie. But most of these cases fit the classic mold which dates back to the early church, Christians who were killed as they lived out their faith by non-Christians. Whether they were killed in the gulags of Russia, by radical Islamic extremists, or by the communist regime in China made no difference, they were martyrs. But left out of the discussion during the papacy of John Paul II were those Christians who were killed during the many civil wars in Latin America. Whether it was to evade delving into politics or because they did not fit the more classic definition, there were no cases of martyrs in twentieth century Latin America being considered for sainthood. Theologians such as Karl Rahner, Johann Baptist Metz, Leonardo Boff, and others began to ask why this was the case. Rahner specifically pointed to Christians killed during World War II and Christians killed in Latin America who were not named as martyrs. Before his death he called for an expanded definition.

During my doctoral studies I also became interested in the question of martyrdom today. After my first research trip to El Salvador, I was captivated by the celebration of the Jesuit martyrs and my visit to the tomb of Oscar Romero. Perhaps most amazing was the reverence that common people had when visiting the garden where the Jesuits were shot, and the prayerful way some kneeled beside or kissed the tomb of Romero in the crypt of the Cathedral. After my second research trip to El Salvador, significant conversations with Jon Sobrino, SJ himself, and after many hours researching and a first attempt to write about the topic the project bore fruit. After Sobrino's insistence that martyrdom was a reality and not a concept, the project bore the finalized title: *The Reality of Martyrdom in the Christology of Jon Sobrino*. Since this first attempt, I have had the opportunity to continue to write and teach on the topic of martyrdom and about Sobrino's Christological work. In addition, with the Beatification of Monseñor Oscar Romero our current Pope Francis has asked theologians to consider how we might allow for an expanded definition for martyrdom in the twenty-first century. This book responds to that challenge of Pope Francis. How do we name Oscar Romero, Rutilio Grande, the U.S. churchwomen, and the Jesuits and the two laywomen killed at the UCA (Universidad Centroamericana) as martyrs? Is it a new category with a new definition? Or is it simply an amplification of what we have long considered Christian witness?

There are a number of studies of the history of martyrdom in the ancient church. Some have even questioned whether or not some of that history might be part mythology and that the church was not as persecuted as some might think. But there can be no doubt that some Christians died at the hands of the Romans, whether as political opponents of the state or those that refused to worship the Roman deities. And over the centuries many men and women have died for their Christian faith. This book does not pretend to offer anything new in terms of the study of martyrdom in the early church, but does briefly discuss this history. But the book does develop the interesting contrast between martyrdom in the early church and martyrdom today with particular focus on Latin America. While there is a long history of martyrdom in Latin America, the primary focus will be to elaborate four case studies for martyrdom today focusing on the reality in El Salvador: Rutilio Grande, SJ killed in 1977, Archbishop Oscar Romero killed in 1980, the U.S. churchwomen killed in 1980, and the six members of the UCA Jesuit community and their two women collaborators killed in 1989.

Insights from the work of Jon Sobrino will illuminate these case studies. First, his Christological insights from *Jesus the Liberator* and *Christ the Liberator* will be used to analyze the reality of martyrdom, particularly in reference to the terms martyr, crucified people, and martyred people. Second, his more recent articles will challenge a strict interpretation of the traditional definition of martyrdom, especially focusing on his terms Jesuanic martyr, a martyr for justice, and even a more controversial suggestion of an anonymous Christian martyr. Finally, the book will conclude by combining Sobrino's insights and the reality of martyrdom today, but updated by the recent scholarship in Romero's beatification process which attempts to show Romero as a martyr. The writing from Romero's beatification process can also be applied to some of the other Salvadoran martyrs.

The reason for using the work of Jon Sobrino is two-fold. First, he escaped death and martyrdom when he was away lecturing, and knows the pain of loss with the deaths of the majority of the Jesuits in his community. He also lived through the Salvadoran Civil War, and saw the impact of the reality of martyrdom. Second, there is a definite shift in his Christology post-1989, and his writings on martyrdom and terminology for the martyrs give the church a broader and more inclusive definition. The fact is in El Salvador, Grande, Romero, etc. are already considered martyrs by the majority of its people. But even though many Salvadorans believe in Romero's cause for sainthood, some still are more hesitant than others to label him a martyr. How is it that a Roman Catholic Archbishop can be shot dead during the celebration of mass by a military sharpshooter who took orders from a purported Roman Catholic officer who operated under the command of a number of Generals, some of whom were purportedly devote Catholics? While this story is indeed unique it impels us toward an answer and demonstrates the need for better terminology and assumption of the reality of martyrdom in Latin America over the past 40 years. In the end the hope is to offer some suggestions for an expanded definition of martyrdom in the twenty-first century. By responding to the call of Pope Francis for an expanded definition, the reality of martyrdom in Latin America might be better understood and applied to the universal church.

Chapter One

The Definition of Martyrdom
Early Martyrdom to Middle Ages

The focus of this exploration will be only on Christian martyrs, even though many religious traditions also have traditions of martyrs. The Jewish tradition before the birth of Christ counts martyrs from the time of the Babylonian captivity, when Hebrew captives were killed for refusing to violate dietary laws by eating pork. And certainly the Maccabees counted as martyrs those who were killed defying Seleucid rule. Additionally, there are martyrs in Islam, which also has a modern twist when considering some who die killing Christians or as part of *jihad* or a holy death. Instead, this search for a definition will be limited to the Christian tradition, and in particular the Roman Catholic tradition, since Orthodox, Lutheran and Anglican traditions also name some as martyrs who were killed by those of Roman Catholic faith. These men and women were killed either intentionally, like many Protestants were killed during the reformation period, or unintentionally, like the Orthodox killed in the Crusades of the Middle Ages, mistaken for Muslim infidels since they spoke Greek or Arabic rather than a European language.

THE SEARCH FOR A DEFINITION

The history of martyrdom finds its roots in nascent Christianity. Tradition holds that almost all of the apostles died for their faith. The Acts of the Apostles relate the tale of the proto-martyr Stephen, and Roman writings document the death of early Christians. From the Cross to the Coliseum, until the acceptance of Christianity by the Roman Empire, thousands of early Christians died for their faith. Patristic authors such as Polycarp and Justin Martyr begin to shape the theological justification for dying for the faith, and early martyrologies recount numerous gruesome deaths in order to honor those who died for their faith. The word martyr comes from the Greek (Μαρτηρ) meaning witness. Simply put, a martyr is a person who dies for the faith. Perpetua, Felicity, and countless others died for their Christian faith.

Larry Cunningham, in *A Brief History of Saints*, outlines the history of the martyrs, what constitutes a martyr, and the resurgence of interest in martyrs today. The history of the martyrs can be traced to the earliest Christian experience. Cunningham writes, "It is an incontestable fact that the early Christian movement suffered persecution at the hands of the authorities of the Roman empire, which continued in fits and starts within the generation after the earthly life of Jesus and continued down until the early fourth century."[1] The severe persecution the Christian community experienced tended to be regional. It wasn't until the third century that Decius insisted upon an Empire wide persecution of the Christian community. The period of the martyrs did not come to a close until the Edict of Toleration issued by the emperor Constantine in Milan in the early fourth century.

An enormous amount of literature bearing upon martyrdom survives from this period. The literature, which began as a response to Roman persecution, takes many forms. Many of the writings took the form of a defense of the Christian faith, that is, an apology. One well-known defense was written by Justin Martyr, who was executed around the year 165. A second kind of literature is known as the *Passio* or the *Martyrium*. This second form of literature can sometimes be termed hagiographical, and some scholars question their veracity.[2] Nevertheless, some of these texts can now be considered classics, such as *The Passion of Perpetua and Felicity*, a third century text which describes the condemnation of a Christian noble woman, Perpetua, and her servant, Felicity. Both were devoured by wild beasts at the circus in Carthage. Another famous text written in the second century is *The Martyrdom of Polycarp*. The text commemorates not only Polycarp but the death of all who suffered martyrdom. The book compares the life of the martyr Polycarp to "the supreme martyr of the Christian faith, Jesus, who died on the cross under a sentence also pronounced by the Roman authorities. The text is written in such a fashion that it is studded with narrative parallels to the passion of Christ. Hence, the martyr's death was seen against the template of the passion of Christ who provides the template for giving up one's life."[3] For those early Christians the proto-martyr is Jesus Christ.

POLYCARP, JESUS AS PROTO-MARTYR

There are many different examples of early Christian martyrs. The martyrdom of Polycarp provides an example of an early Christian martyr who was venerated by many, and is an example of literature that attempts to show Jesus as Proto-martyr as well.[4] Saint Polycarp (ca. 69–ca. 155) was a second century bishop of Smyrna, an ancient Greek city located at a central and strategic point on the Aegean coast of Anatolia and known today as Izmir, Turkey.[5] He died a martyr when he was stabbed after an attempt to burn him at the stake failed. Polycarp is recognized as a saint in the Roman Catholic, Eastern Orthodox, Anglican, and Lutheran churches. With Clement of Rome and Ignatius of Antioch, Polycarp is considered one of three chief Apostolic Fathers. The Letter of the Martyrdom of Polycarp purports to have been written by the Church at Smyrna to the Church at Philomelium, and through that Church to the whole Christian world, in order to give a succinct account of the circumstances attending the martyrdom of Polycarp. It is one of the earliest of all the *Martyria*, and has generally been considered the most interesting and authentic. The letter describes the martyrdom of Polycarp, as well as providing a path of resistance to those who followed the teachings of the bishop "who put an end to the persecution, having, as it were, set a seal upon it by his martyrdom. For almost all the events that happened previously [to this one] took place that the Lord might show us from above a martyrdom becoming the Gospel."[6] The letter makes the claim that all martyrdom is blessed and noble especially when conforming to the will of God.

Polycarp purportedly had a premonition in a vision of his own martyrdom. He envisioned himself burning alive before it actually happened. When he was arrested, he was asked to renounce his faith, but he claimed he could not saying, "Eighty and six years have I served Him, and He never did me any injury: how then can I blaspheme my King and my Savior?"[7] He was in fact burned alive for confessing to the crime of Christianity. The author writes,

> When the fire was ready, and he had divested himself of all his clothes and unfastened his belt, he tried to take off his shoes, though he was not heretofore in the habit of doing this because the faithful always vied with one another as to which of them would be first to touch his body. For he had always been honored, even before his martyrdom, for his holy life. Straightway then, they set about him the material prepared for the pyre. And when they were about to nail him also, he said: "Leave me as I am. For he who grants me to endure the fire will enable me also to remain on the pyre unmoved, without the security you desire from the nails."[8]

The letter hopes to inspire other Christian witnesses through the example of Polycarp.

Early Christians often revered the martyrs as models of exemplary faith. Cunningham describes the veneration of the martyrs when he writes, "There is no doubt that those who did die for the sake of the faith were highly venerated in the Christian community. The literature that grew up about them is proof enough of that fact."[9] St. Polycarp was one of those venerated martyrs. Early Christians venerated Polycarp's tomb in order to remember his commitment and sacrifice for the Christian community. This veneration of martyrs paralleled in some respects Roman cultural practices. Pagans worshiped their ancestors, and the Romans customarily memorialized their dead on an annual basis. Christians later added the idea of a martyr's "birthday," the day which they entered into heaven. The text of the martyrdom of Polycarp reminded Christians to observe the cult of the martyrs and thereby more perfectly imitate Jesus as disciples. The cult of martyrs developed so extensively that,

> By the middle of the fourth century, we have a list of those martyrs who were commemorated in Rome on an annual basis (the so-called *Deposito Martyrum*) with similar lists compiled in cities like Antioch and Carthage. It is from this practice that, in time, there developed a cycle of saintly veneration that meshed with the larger liturgical cycle of the church. One scholar has pointed out the Roman *Deposito Martyrum* begins, fittingly enough, on December 25 with the birthday of Jesus—the model for all Christian martyrs.[10]

The venerated martyrs find their center in the proto-martyr—Jesus. This will become important for those who want to demonstrate that early Christians originally venerated Jesus as a martyr. The humanity of Jesus was emphasized to show that he truly did die on the cross, and was an inspiration to other Christians, who were also willing to die for their faith.

It should be noted that recent scholarship has questioned the veracity of some of the early accounts of martyrdom. In her book *Ancient Christian Martyrdom*, Candida Moss examines many of the ancient traditions of martyrdom from Asia Minor to Rome, and North Africa to Alexandria.[11] She notes that the process by which Christians were killed rarely occurred by decree but happened idiosyncratically. Martyrdom did become a part of Christian identity and "was also an important cultural influence in the formation of the Christian canon."[12] In addition evidence suggests that some of the early accounts of the martyrs were not eyewitness accounts. For example, Moss claims that the martyrdom of Polycarp is likely not an eyewitness account but instead a fusion of the historical with the Christ figure and the ideal of a Greek hero.[13] But in the end Moss herself concedes that "Whether ancient Christians suffered prolonged agonies in the arena or long lives bearing the burdens of self-restraint, their bodies were shaped by these ideologies of martyrdom."[14] Whether completely historically accurate or not, these early accounts of the martyrs shaped early Christian faith and piety, and continue to do so today. In a more recent work, Moss suggests that some of the mythology of the martyrs can also lead to a myth of widespread persecution which can inhibit the ability of Christians to openly dialog with those of different faiths.[15] But one can honor the memory of the martyrs by focusing on their virtues, so as to avoid the creation of an antagonistic dichotomy between those of differing faiths or opinions.

MARTYRDOM AFTER CONSTANTINE

After Constantine the veneration of the martyrs continued as a well-established part of Christian life. Cunningham writes, "Constantine himself paid fair tribute to the practice by, among other things, underwriting the erection of a large basilica over the tomb of Saint Peter on the site of the shrine (tropheum) where his remains were venerated."[16] The veneration of the martyrs would later shift to a veneration of martyrs and saints. But if one wanted to categorize history into ideal types then the first four centuries comprised the age of the martyrs. Prayers and litanies surrounded the veneration of the martyrs, and their relics were thought to hold a sacred power. In the *Life of Polycarp*, for example, the martyrs' relics are characterized as more precious than gems or gold. While the age of the martyrs may have come to an end by the end of the fourth century, their veneration continued, and the devotion transferred to the ascetic saints. When Christianity became the religion of the state and persecution ended, moves to address more doctrinal concerns shifted the focus from surviving as a church and from the age of the martyrs. Logically then, the martyrs were remembered by some Patristic authors, but martyrdom itself was not a pressing concern. The church had simply moved on to address other needs and concerns. Augustine, for instance, does examine the issue of martyrdom, but only cursorily.[17] In the middle ages, Thomas Aquinas only briefly treats the issue of the martyrs—for example with his mention of the Holy Innocents. His views will be examined later when discussing Karl Rahner's and Leonardo Boff's opinions concerning martyrdom.

At the end of the Middle Ages and the beginning of the Catholic Reformation there is a resurgence in the number of martyrs. On the Catholic side of the Reformation, a number of martyrs are added to the books, after being put to death at the hands of Protestants, with the English martyrs who died at the hands of the Anglican head of state among the most famous. St. Thomas More may be the most well-known example, but Roman Catholics in Britain were killed in large numbers. Priests, who were forbidden to live in England, nevertheless came to minister to the Catholic faithful. Robert Southwell, Edmund Campion, and other Jesuit priests and brothers died in this period, and were later declared Saints or Blesseds and Martyrs.[18] While some Catholics were martyred at the hands of the Protestant Reformers, many more died in the missions, especially in the Far East and the Americas. The Jesuits, Dominicans and Franciscans all claim large numbers of saintly martyrs in this period. In the Americas, we find examples of the North American martyrs in New France who died at the hands of the Iroquois. Jean de Brebeuf, Isaac Jogues and companions all died as Christian martyrs during this missionary expansion. Large numbers of Catholic Christians were also killed in India, Indochina, and Japan during this time.

Another place where martyrdom was real as well as prolific was in the Jesuit reductions of South America. These Jesuit reductions or missions were recently made famous by the movie "The Mission,"[19] and many Jesuits were killed as they attempted to bring Christianity to the new Spanish and Portuguese territories in Peru for the Spanish and Brazil for the Portuguese. These missions originally were utilized as a means of pacification especially by the Dominican and Franciscan priests and brothers who first accompanied Spanish militias to the Americas. The aggressive missionary effort brought Christianity to many different parts of the "new" world. But the Jesuits were able to create something different, a fusion of cultures, in which no European persons other than the missionaries were allowed to enter these indigenous territories.[20] In all cases, whether the forced "conversion" by the sword or the more utopian Jesuit vision, the encounter with new tribes still provoked hostility—and in the end producing martyrs.

As noted in the introduction, this chapter will not delve into the myriad of martyrs from other faiths and Christian denominations. Our Jewish brothers and sisters count the Maccabean period as one when many died for their faith, and in modern times the Holocaust saw many witnesses. Our Orthodox brothers and sisters also have a separate but notable martyrology, which differed even before the split with Rome. And our Protestant brothers and sisters count as their martyrs, starting from the time of Luther, Calvin, and Zwingli, the many who died for their Protestant faiths in Germany and Switzerland, and as they grew as Christian denominations throughout the world.

NOTES

1. Cunningham, Lawrence S. *A Brief History of Saints*. Malden, MA: Blackwell Publishing, 2005, 11. For another great source for early Christian martyrs see Musurillo, Herbert. *Acts of the Christian Martyrs*. Vol. 2. New York: Oxford University Press, 1972.

2. See the recent work of Moss, Candida. *Ancient Christian Martyrdom: Diverse Practices, Theologies, and Traditions*. New Haven: Yale University Press, 2012.

3. *A Brief History of Saints*, 15.

4. For brevity's sake I will not examine the life of Justin Martyr, and instead focus on Polycarp. For those who would want to use Justin Martyr as a second example, see the *Early Church Fathers Series* Volume One which gives ample information on his life and writings.

5. For more on the biography of Polycarp see online sources, Wikipedia or New Advent. See also Richardson, Cyril C., ed. *Early Christian Fathers*. Vol. 1. New York: MacMillan Publishing Co. Inc., 1970.

6. *Early Christian Fathers*, 149.

7. *Early Christian Fathers*, 152.

8. Ibid, 154.

9. *A Brief History of Saints*, 16.

10. *A Brief History of Saints*, 17.

11. Moss, Candida. *Ancient Christian Martyrdom: Diverse Practices, Theologies and Traditions*. New Haven: Yale University Press, 2012.

12. *Ancient Christian Martyrdom*, 13.

13. Ibid, 76.

14. Ibid, 167.

15. Moss, Candida. *The Myth of Persecution: How Early Christians Invented a Story of Martyrdom*. New York: Harper Collins Publishers, 2013.

16. *A Brief History of Saints*, 19.

17. Cunningham develops this whole history more fully in his work. While I will not take the time to develop Augustine's thoughts on martyrdom, one should note that a number of authors have written on Augustine's perspective.

18. Robert Southwell and Edmund Campion are the most well-known martyrs from this period, but hundreds of Catholics were put to death in this period for refusing to accept Anglicanism or the King as the head of the church. For examples of the Protestant martyrs during this period, see Cunningham's *A Brief History of Saints*, especially pages 68–71 and the discussion of the Anabaptists in England, and the Quakers in the United States.

19. The movie centered on the Jesuit reductions with the Guarani in modern day Paraguay, Brazil and Argentina, but the model for the reductions extended throughout South America, and the system of the reductions extended from modern day Peru, through Bolivia, Paraguay, Argentina, and southern Brazil, and included many different tribes. One of the most famous Paraguayan martyrs is San Roque Gonzalez. His heart is kept in the Jesuit church in Asunción, and is still an object of veneration today. David Block has an interesting study of the Moxos reductions in Bolivia entitled *Mission Culture on the Upper Amazon*. Frederick Reiter writes a history of the Paraguayan Jesuit mission in *They Built Utopia*, to cite just two of the numerous sources.

20. One example of this unique fusion can still be visited today, in the Moxos region of Bolivia. Surviving because of its remote geography, the Jesuits returned to this region in the early 1980s. Don Doll, SJ and I collaborated on an article with photos for the *Yearbook of the Society of Jesus 2015* entitled "Living Reminders of a Heroic Age."

Chapter Two

Martyrdom in Contemporary Times

The twentieth century brings with it a new breed of martyr, the one who fights for justice, and who most often does so against a government or oppressive regime.[1] Miguel Pro, SJ serves as an example of one whose death as a martyr for justice has been recognized by his subsequent beatification as Blessed Miguel Pro. The case for a new typology of martyrs comes primarily from the past century. Cunningham writes, "It has been argued by more than one scholar that more Christians died because they were Christians in the twentieth century than all those who died over the course of the three centuries of Roman persecution."[2] Some of these Christians died in violent attacks: Christians who died in the Russian gulags, Polish priests killed in concentration camps in World War II Germany, or Christians suppressed in China, Japan, and India, or Islamic countries such as Albania. But a new phenomenon seen in the last century also includes violence against Roman Catholic Christians in purportedly Roman Catholic countries.

Throughout Latin America many Christians have died at the hands of their fellow Christian brothers and sisters, often for political ideology and not Christian tenets. While these men and women died defending their beliefs, they were not martyrs in the same sense as those Christians killed as gladiators in the Coliseum or as innocents fed to the lions for sport by the Romans. That is to say, they were Christians killed by non-Christians. Cunningham asserts, "In the Roman world the case for martyrdom was clear. Christians suffered and died because in the minds of the Romans they did not show pietas to the Roman pantheon of gods and in that refusal, seemed to be a treacherous fifth column undermining the legitimacy of the Roman state. . . In our times, the matter is more complex."[3] Because the matter is complex, one must question whether or not an expanded definition of martyrdom is helpful. Cunningham raises but does not answer this question, "Finally, were those lay people, religious sisters, priests, and bishops (like Oscar Romero) who were assassinated by the death squads in El Salvador Christian martyrs or the targets of political assassins?"[4] One could say that they were martyrs in a broad sense. One could make the claim on the grounds that they did witness against injustice and calumny against them, and sought to love others in the midst of regimes or political instruments of destruction and hate.

Some theologians want to broaden the concept of martyrdom. Theologians as early as Thomas Aquinas and as recently as Karl Rahner have asked for a more generous understanding of martyrdom, especially to encompass what is at the very least a complex response to a death that encapsulates a Thomistic sense of fortitude, faith, and love, into a willingness to die for truth. Our modern times may lead us to look for new definitions as Christians continue to die for their faith. In fact, Cunningham sets down a number of categories for such definitions which could be termed "Rahner's challenge." Cunningham enumerates,

> Following up on Rahner's challenge, some contemporary commentators have set out expanded criteria for the assessment of martyrdom. They generally indicate three such criteria: (1) The person must have been executed or died as a direct result of mistreatment; (2) the person responsible for the death must have either had a hatred for the faith of some virtues annexed to, and flowing from the faith; and (3) the putative martyr must have had some sense that his or her activities might well cost them persecution at a minimum with the probability of death. Even using those criteria one must act with subtlety and discrimination.[5]

Pope John Paul II also argued for a broadened sense of the term. Of the hundreds canonized during his papacy, one finds many examples of martyrs, both traditional and non-traditional. In his 1995 encyclical, *Ut Unum Sint*, he writes, "In a theocentric vision, we Christians already have a common martyrology. This also includes the martyrs of the present century, more common than one might think, and it shows at a profound level, God preserves communion among the baptized in the supreme demand of faith, manifested in the sacrifice of life itself."[6] Pope John Paul II also provides a number of interesting cases, from a variety of continents. Edith Stein and the religious killed during the Spanish Civil War are just two examples from Europe, as well as those World War II priests killed in the concentration camps in Germany and Poland. Those killed in the Russian gulags during and after World War II also warrant further consideration; though with a communist government one can still make a case that they fit a more traditional definition. In this case, if the government is truly atheist they would fit the definition of Christians being killed by non-Christians.

There are many martyrs who die for their beliefs, and some prophetically. The Latin American context, for example, produces a large number of cases of men and women who die for their prophetic stance. For example, "Those who did die precisely as Christians protesting the inhumanity of tyrannical political systems function as prophetic figures who stood for the teachings of Jesus against either the passivity of those who acquiesced to regnant power (Nazi Germany) . . . or as solitary figures who made up a small voice in a near totally hostile culture (the Christian minority in Pakistan)."[7] Sobrino provides a helpful term Jesuanic, and the designation "Jesuanic martyr" for one who dies like Jesus, at the hands of some hostile force. This term encompasses those who actively died for their beliefs, as well as the more passive martyrs who simply disappeared or who remain nameless. While Pope John Paul II may not have accepted the idea of the nameless martyr, he was keen on promoting martyrs who died witnessing to the Gospel truths, even if it expanded the traditional idea of what constitutes a martyr. He mentions Polish priests who died for their faith in prison, and also spoke about the death of Father Jerzy Popieluszko, the priest who died in the Solidarity movement, and whose grave site today is venerated and honored as a martyr's shrine.[8]

Cunningham makes the case for expanding the traditional definition of a martyr. He notes that Romero's grave in El Salvador is already venerated, and many considered him a saint long before his beatification. He remarks, "Martyrs like Romero and others have clearly understood that allegiance to the faith in places where this allegiance could mean their death at the hands of the political powers entailed a different kind of martyrdom and a different kind of Christian witness. Such persons were living in a kind of postmodern world in which the lingering echoes of the old Christian order were only present in shadowy and vague forms of sentimentality."[9] But examples of this different kind of martyr continue even in our present day. The Sicilian priest who is killed while trying to reconcile different mafia factions, the priest beheaded and made an example of in India, the Jesuit superior of the Russian region murdered in Moscow: all of these cases beg for an expanded understanding of martyrdom. In his essay on the *Universal Call to Holiness*, John Paul II seems to agree. He argues that the martyr is the one who willingly risks his or her life itself as a witness to immutable truth and as a witness to Christian love and charity.[10] He sees the martyr as a testimony against the horrors of the age and a sign of hope for those who resist the culture of death in contemporary life, serving as a moral witness. These considerations thus raise the question: Are the Jesuanic martyr, the martyr of Rahner's challenge, and the martyr of Christian charity, in fact one and the same?

MARTYRDOM TODAY

In response to this question it is useful to recall that the movement to expand the concept of martyrdom began in a 1983 book entitled *Martyrdom Today*, in which Johann Baptist Metz and Edward Schillebeeckx edited a set of essays revisiting the topic of martyrdom. In this book, Karl Rahner called for just such an expansion in his essay on martyrdom, written just one year before his death. Rahner's essay makes a plea to broaden the concept of martyrdom. He begins by affirming that the traditional concept of martyrdom is not in dispute, and is in fact well known. He writes, "Here we presuppose the concept of martyrdom that is traditional in the Church today: what is meant by this concept of dogmatic and fundamental theology is the free, tolerant acceptance of death for the sake of the faith, except in the course of an active struggle as in the case of soldiers."[11] Rahner wants to make a distinction between martyrdom and simple fighting, since the traditional concept of martyrdom accepts only the martyr who dies as an act of faith and not one who dies in military service. But Rahner does want to explore the concept of martyrdom in the face of some worthy struggles. He takes the life of Jesus as an example when he writes,

> First of all, the death Jesus passively endured was the consequence of the struggle he waged against those in his day who wielded religious and political power. He died because he fought: his death must not be seen in isolation from his life. Putting this argument the other way around, someone who dies while fighting actively for the demands of his or her Christian convictions can also be said patiently to endure his or her death. It is not a death directly sought in itself. It includes a passive element, just as the death of a martyr in the usual sense includes an active element since by his or her active witness and life this kind of martyr has conjured up the situation in which he or she can only escape death by denying his or her faith.[12]

For Rahner, the action of martyrdom is important, but so is the intention. A martyr might die for the faith, but they may not intend to. Their active witness is not a suicidal intention, but one which takes place as a consequence of their faith. Rahner is also careful to note that not every Christian who dies in a religious war dies as a martyr.[13]

What Rahner really wants us to examine is the situation in Latin America. What happens when Roman Catholic Christians are killing fellow Catholic Christians? He asks the question, "But, for example, why should not someone like Bishop Romero, who died while fighting for justice in society, a struggle he waged out of the depths of his conviction as a Christian—why should he not be a martyr? Certainly he was prepared for his death."[14] In this question he shifts the focus from the traditional idea of what constitutes a martyr. The modern problematic brings an inconceivable case: A Christian bishop killed by soldiers, ordered by a lieutenant and perhaps even a general who were purportedly devout Catholics. Rahner affirms, "We should not simply conceive of passively tolerating one's death only in the manner we are used to in the case of early Christian martyrs brought before a court and sentenced to death. There are quite different ways in which the passive but intentionally accepted toleration of death can occur."[15] What Rahner further points out as strange are the cases of contemporary Christians who have not been judicially sentenced to death, and sometimes are even killed anonymously. Many of those killed in Latin America, religious, priests and laity, who were never sentenced in a court serve as examples here. They were systematically slain. These anonymous forms of death clash with the more classical definition of a martyr.[16]

The situation in Latin America provokes theologians to answer the following question: What happens when Roman Catholic Christians are killing fellow Christians? When Rahner asks the question why Romero should not be a martyr, he shifts the focus from the traditional idea of what constitutes a martyr. The killing of Romero brings an inconceivable case: A Roman Catholic bishop killed by soldiers, ordered by a lieutenant and perhaps even a general with the permission of the President of a country who were purportedly devout Catholics. This modern problematic calls for an expanded understanding of what it means to be a martyr since these forms of death clash with mainline early Christian understanding of what constitutes a martyr.[17]

Rahner sees these more complicated cases as qualifying for martyrdom. He takes a case familiar to him when he remarks, "What is in fact strange is that the Church has canonized Maximillian Kolbe as a confessor and not a martyr.[18] An unprejudiced approach would pay more attention to how he behaved in the concentration camp and at his death than to his earlier life and would see him as a martyr of selfless Christian love."[19] Rahner admits it is difficult to distinguish between an active struggle which leads to death for the faith, and a more passive endurance which leads to martyrdom. What the two cases hold in common is that both explicitly and decidedly accepted death for Christian reasons. Both Kolbe and Romero accepted death. Just as Jesus Christ died in a supreme act of love and fortitude they also reveal God's love. For Rahner, this action evidences a deep belief in God, but also our extreme helplessness when we attempt to follow Jesus and accept the cross. In his plea for broadening the concept of martyrdom, Rahner appeals to St. Thomas Aquinas. He claims that Thomas would define a martyr as someone who is clearly related to Christ because he or she is defending society against the attacks of enemies of the Christian faith. When those enemies are trying to damage the Christian faith, and the Christian suffers death, she is a martyr.[20]

Rahner suggests a clear path for political and liberation theologians when he implies that they should work toward enlarging this concept of martyrdom, and that the concept has practical significance: a responsibility for peace and justice in the world. Liberation theologians take a further step with this practical significance, since for many in Latin America martyrdom is not just a concept, but a reality.

Leonardo Boff and Jon Sobrino follow Rahner's lead to broadening the concept of martyrdom. Boff tackles martyrdom from a systematic perspective. Similar to Cunningham, Boff begins with a historical approach to martyrdom, and views Jesus as the proto-martyr. Boff echoes St. Augustine, when he claims "not the punishment but the cause makes the martyr."[21] The resurrection of Jesus holds theological significance for the martyr since whoever loses her life, receives life in fullness. Boff claims, "to the martyr is reserved full participation in the meaning of life, that is, enthronement in its immortal kingdom."[22] Boff advocates the examination of the preaching of Jesus to find the main elements of martyrdom. The gospels affirm that we will be hated for the sake of the kingdom, and dragged before governors and teachers. The Beatitudes tell us that those who are persecuted for the sake of following Jesus Christ will be blessed in heaven.

For the early Christians, martyrdom occurred because they followed the teachings of Jesus Christ. Because of this Christian discipleship, Boff emphasizes the subversive nature of early Christianity. He claims, "So the Christian faith became politically subversive, since it attacked the foundations of the political-religious apparatus of the Empire and its leaders."[23] Thus, Boff hopes to stretch the ancient definition of martyr and apply it to modern times. Just as the early martyrs died for their faith because of their practice of the faith, so too do Christians today die for their faith. He claims that many Christians in the third world continue to carry out actions based in faith and the Gospel message. He asserts, "Not a few Christians . . . because of the Gospel, make a preferential option for the poor, for their liberation for the defence of their rights. In the name of this option they stand up and denounce the exercise of domination and all forms of social dehumanisation. They may be persecuted arrested, tortured and killed. They too are martyrs in the strict sense of the word."[24] Like Rahner, Boff appeals to Thomas, claiming that any human good can be the cause of martyrdom, in so far as it is oriented to God. For Boff, the numerous Christians who die for their faith in the attempt to liberate their brothers and follow Jesus Christ are no less martyrs than those who confessed their faith before a Roman tribunal and joyfully accepted their death.

In a 1983 essay Sobrino takes a slightly different approach to martyrdom, viewing it from the perspective of political holiness. He argues that holiness has a place in the political sphere, and uses Monseñor Romero as a concrete example of this holiness. He claims this kind of political holiness is derived from the call of the episcopal conferences at Medellín and Puebla. The response to this call is love, and the response to the enormous number of people suffering he terms political love. Sobrino writes, "This political love has certain specific characteristics which differentiates it from other forms of love. In this first place it requires a *metanoia* to see the truth of the world as it is, in the manifestations of death, which are visible, and its structural causes, which are hidden and care to be hidden, to see in this generalised death the largest fact and the most serious problem of humanity."[25] For Sobrino political love necessitates a conversion of heart, but also an awareness of the surrounding suffering. Political love then calls for a response, an attempt to transform the world around the lover. When performed correctly this love is poured out, a *kenosis*, which leads to recognition of the world of the poor. Conversion of heart leads to loving action to change the plight of the poor.

The expression of political love also makes a person subject to persecution. Sobrino claims, "This is the inexorable fulfilment of Jesus's preaching. Political love, unlike other forms of love, unleashes the specific suffering of persecution by all the powers of this world. Not all Christians, but political Christians are attacked, vilified, threatened, expelled, arrested, tortured and murdered."[26] In this essay on political holiness, Sobrino does make a personal call to action. But he does not characterize these political Christians who die for their faith explicitly as martyrs. He cites Romero as an example of political holiness, but stops short of characterizing him as a martyr. However, he does make the claim for political saints. He writes, "Political saints are a reality. Suffering peoples recognise as saints those who embody themselves through love in the political and they only recognise as saints of today those who take the risks of this incarnation. This may be done in different ways and the sacrifice of their lives is their ultimate justification."[27] Sobrino acknowledges the holy sacrifice of Jean Donovan and the U.S. women missionaries, and the ministerial work of Mons. Romero, two of the case studies to be examined in chapter 4. He also recognizes that this form of sainthood does not necessarily coincide with what the church means by holiness or the process of canonization. But Sobrino does insist that this gift of political holiness, this sacrificing sanctity, does come from God. He ends with a famous quotation from Romero, "Brothers, I rejoice that our Church is persecuted because it has chosen the poor and because it has tried to become incarnate with the poor."[28]

RETHINKING MARTYRDOM

Twenty years later, Sobrino edited a response to the book *Martyrdom Today*, in a Concilium edition entitled *Rethinking Martyrdom*. This book revisits the Concilium articles of 1983 taking on the task of re-characterizing what constitutes a martyr. Surprisingly twenty years after the first volume these articles show that the world as a whole remains cruel. Ethnic conflicts, poverty and oppression produce people who respond with mercy "and for this reason they are violently and unjustly killed without being able to mount any defence."[29] Those who die from within the Christian tradition will be called "Jesus martyrs" because "they die like Jesus, and because they have lived, worked and struggled as he did."[30] Second, this Concilium edition shows the effects of suicide and terrorism in our world. The fanaticism of suicide can generate an extreme sort of ambiguity in what consists of a martyr. One could call into question whether a church that speaks about martyrs is on the side of the victims or the victimizers. Third, this edition gives a name to the "crucified peoples" a term which Sobrino borrows from his brother Jesuit Ignacio Ellacuría, murdered at the UCA Jesuit University in San Salvador in 1989. Crucial to his discussion is the issue of whether or not the deaths of millions of human beings due to poverty, war, hunger and AIDS are being taken seriously by church and society. Sobrino will argue that those who give up their lives in the attempt to take these people down from the cross may be named martyrs. In this way, "if we take the 'Jesus martyrs' and the 'crucified peoples' together, this martyrial reality provides the world with light, hope and an appeal."[31]

While we normally associate martyrdom with early Christians, violence in Latin America has produced a new phenomenon. The twentieth century can be characterized as a time of suffering, and both victims and victimizers rise to the forefront. In this new reality some are moved to compassion. As Sobrino asserts, "there are people who, faced with victims, react and defend them in various ways—solidarity movements, human rights movements, anti-globalization protests—and sometimes do so to the very end."[32] Bluntly, many times those who defend the victims, wind up dying for their compassionate action. These deaths are sometimes not the same as the traditional definition of the martyr. That is to say, sometimes their deaths do not occur directly in the course of "witnessing to the faith." For this reason Sobrino makes a bold claim:

> In our time, "martyrdom" has, then, taken on a new form. Many men and women have suffered violent deaths not on account of their witness to faith but because of the compassion that stems from their faith. In the church, these have been bishops and sisters, catechists and delegates of the word; in civil society, they have ranged from peasants and indigenous inhabitants to students, lawyers, and journalists. In one way and another, they have unmasked the lie used to cover over the death of the poor and have struggled against injustice. They have been people of compassion against cruelty.[33]

But one might also address the need to account for the hundreds of thousands of human beings who have been slaughtered without the chance to flee. He cites as examples, El Mozote in El Salvador, the genocide in Rwanda, and the millions of refugees who live in permanent destitution which leads to death. This new historical context forces us to rethink a narrow interpretation of martyrdom. The Vatican II concept of "the signs of the times" applies to the concept of martyrdom in the Third World. We need to read these signs in the light of Christian witness in Latin America today.

Sobrino acknowledges the semantic problem of applying the concept of martyrdom to this new situation. He remarks, "To describe the individual victims we have made *novel* use of the traditional term 'martyr.'"[34] People in El Salvador immediately used the terms pastor and martyr to describe Romero at the time of his death. Martyrdom could be seen in Romero in a true sense, a man who died for a greater love of God's people. But neither Church nor society has a word for the second group, those who were massacred violently or experienced a lingering death. Comparing them to the Holy Innocents does not do them justice. Romero called these people "the pierced Christ."[35] This allusion to Christ, is the same allusion Ellacuría implies with his term "the crucified people" which Sobrino utilizes liberally in his analysis of what constitutes a martyr. For Sobrino a martyr is also one who dies for those more anonymous, those who are "crucified" or suffer every single day.

Sobrino adds to the mix when he coins the term "Jesus martyrs." Again, alluding to early Christian understanding of Jesus as first martyr, he accounts for the novelty of the Latin American reality. Sobrino claims, "Those men and women who have given their lives out of reactive compassion for the victims recall Jesus."[36] There is a distinction made between simply loving the poor and the marginalized through works of charity, and actually defending them by giving up one's life. In this way these martyrs are in fact "Jesus martyrs" because they die like Jesus and their following Jesus leads them to suffer a violent death. For this reason, "Jesus martyrs are not, strictly speaking, those who die for Christ, but those who die like Jesus and for the cause of Jesus. Their martyrdom does not result from fidelity to some mandate of Jesus's, or even from a desire for mystical identification with the crucified Jesus, but arises out of their effective following of Jesus."[37] Just as Jesus served as a witness to the truth so too do the "Jesus martyrs" witness to the truth. Their martyrdom is not produced out of *odium fidei* but out of a sense of compassion which leads them to a greater love. For this reason "These martyrs can be martyrs *in* the church, but they are not martyrs *of* the church."[38] One has to go back to St. Thomas Beckett to recall a case similar to that of Archbishop Romero. But "Thomas was killed for defending the rights, legitimate or otherwise, *of the church*, whereas Romero was killed for placing himself *on the side of the poor*."[39] So the reasons for giving preference to the theological concepts of martyrdom are not only historical but theological. By relating the "Jesus martyrs" to the reality of Jesus Christ, they become "a hermeneutical principle, a mystagogy, for understanding the martyrdom of Jesus."[40]

Martyrdom and the crucified peoples must be closely linked. For now, suffice it to say that Sobrino will push for a new definition for the masses. In his words, "Calling these masses 'crucified people' and 'suffering servant of Yahweh' is an act of reparation that should have taken place a long time ago. . . . It means not only conferring dignity on the dead but seeing a saving power in them."[41] Sobrino argues that by naming all of those peoples who died anonymously, we both dignify their deaths, and in doing so take their lives and their reality seriously.

By following Sobrino's lead to its natural end, one can show a direct link between the "Jesus martyrs" and the "crucified peoples." However, Sobrino himself questions which of the two is "more martyr." By asking the question, Sobrino sets up an interesting problematic, but he never fully answers the question. He simply suggests that "there are *two basic types* of unjust violent death, both of supreme historical importance and supreme Christian excellence."[42] By introducing these two types of martyrs, he accounts for those nameless people who were oppressed during their lifetimes, and massacred in death.

> Whether they are called "martyrs" or not—those human beings on whom God looks with infinite tenderness in their suffering, even before considering their personal or moral situation (Puebla n. 1142)—though they often have the basic holiness of living and laying down their lives so that all the poor may be reached by just a little life. Nevertheless, over them there descends an inhuman and anti-Christian silence, while the great ones of this world, including the saints are exalted—"eliteistly" if I may be allowed the word—in a way that a Francis of Assisi or Romero of America would be the first to condemn.[43]

Sobrino makes obvious the need to rethink what constitutes being a martyr. But it is not possible to separate the individual from the masses. Sobrino claims that this is not only wrong but dangerous. If we concentrate only on a few exceptional martyrs, "we abandon the crucified people to their fate."[44] Rethinking martyrdom goes beyond seeking new definitions. It also makes us rethink our world, and to ask ourselves "whether the cries of the crucified people have reached us and whether the Jesus martyrs move us to compassion."[45]

Compassion for the crucified peoples leads Sobrino to make an appeal. He wants to include both the Jesus Martyrs and the Crucified People in his definition of what constitutes a martyr. In doing so, Sobrino makes a methodological move toward the incarnational. He wants to confess a Jesus who is present, not distant, from the people. When the church confesses that Christ is present in the Eucharist, it also confesses that Christ is present in the word, in its pastors, and in its community. Sobrino affirms Matthew 25 by claiming "there is a final bastion of the presence of God and his Christ: 'And with particular tenderness he chose to identify himself with those who are poorest and weakest.'"[46] The poor too embody the presence of Christ. The poor can also be good news, evangelizers, and a *metanoia*, a call to conversion. Simply put, "They are the presence of Christ."[47]

Some Latin American theologians want to push the definition of martyrdom a step further. Sobrino claims, "The poor and their clamors reach their highest expression in the martyrs—in the Jesus martyrs and above all the crucified peoples—and this is what gives the greatest capacity for appealing to the church."[48] In terms of numbers, the Jesus martyrs and the crucified peoples cannot be ignored. In addition, the horrors which they experience spur us to conversion. The appeal of the Jesus martyrs may be made more concrete at specific moments in history. But their appeal lives on in our collective memories. Sobrino hopes that this appeal comes from the victims themselves, and that "this basic appeal will relate not to just anything but to the essence of Christian faith: mercy, love, defence of the poor, and identification with the victims."[49] But this appeal could lead one to ask if it comes from Jesus, or whether it "follows Jesus in his incarnation, mission, cross and resurrection."[50] Sobrino will analyze this "seguimiento" or following of Jesus in four different ways.

The first appeal relates to the incarnation of Jesus Christ. Sobrino questions whether the church really wants to encounter the real and whether or not his appeal corresponds to the incarnation of Jesus. He claims, "This incarnation is not easy for the church, even though, according to its faith, it is an obvious and primary requirement. John's prologue expresses the *will of God* himself *to be real* in our world, a will that consists not simply in becoming actual flesh but in becoming weak flesh."[51] In some ways it is easier for the church to simply remain in the ethereal realm, and not touch the reality of many. But for Sobrino, avoiding the reality of so many people verges on the heretical. Sobrino asserts, "For the church (and not just for christology), the greatest problem here is *docetism* (Walter Kasper), that is creating its own sphere of reality (doctrinal, liturgical, canonical), which distances it and so defends it from the real world, and above all from its crosses."[52] Emphasizing the divinity of Jesus allows the church to forget about the weak human flesh of the incarnate Word, this flesh which died on the cross. The challenge becomes whether or not we can overcome the lethargic sleep of docetism. The role of the martyrs proves to be the key factor to overcoming this sense of complacency. The answer to the challenge comes from the cry of the poor themselves. Sobrino writes, "The miracle can be worked by the crucified peoples, who are crying out with inexpressible cries and calling us to come down. And the Jesus martyrs, who provide an example of doing so."[53]

Jesus martyrs such as Martin Luther King, Archbishop Romero, and even Ignacio Ellacuría can show the way. We remember Romero's words that a church which stands with the preferential option for the poor becomes incarnate in the concerns of the poor, and witnesses to a church incarnate in the people's problems. Sobrino allows for the fact that even Romero's church has its limitations of error and sinfulness, and that overcoming our "docetistic" tendency does not happen easily. But, "The martyrs appeal to us and encourage us to move beyond it (our docetism): the crucified peoples themselves are a call for us to open our eyes to reality, the Jesus martyrs show us how to get involved in it."[54] The martyrs show us a way to act in response to the call of the crucified, and help us rescue the humanity of Christ evidenced in the New Testament.

Sobrino's second appeal points toward a mission of compassion. Sobrino rescues two aspects of the liberating message of Paul VI and the episcopal conference at Medellín. The first concerns *"the salvation of a whole people."*[55] Sobrino sees the role of Romero as someone who was sent by God to save everyone, rich and poor. Sobrino stresses, "the *ultimate purpose* of mission, which covers and embraces all aspects of the life and dignity of the oppressed majorities: the kingdom of God, the human family."[56] Also, the church must reclaim its prophetic stance in proclaiming both the kingdom and the anti-kingdom. There are forces which work against the mission of the church, so the church must proclaim the Good News in a fashion which exposes those parts of society which work against this mission, this good news. In addition, the church must continue to struggle on behalf of the majority, the poor. If not, the church will become "a closed sect or, indeed, a massive institution, but one detached from reality, a new attempt at socio-cultural Christendom."[57] A prophetic pathos encourages church members to respond compassionately to the crucified peoples. Otherwise the discourse of the preferential option for the poor ends with empty platitudes.

Sobrino emphasizes the cross in order to take on the burden of the reality in his third appeal. He claims, "Reality is a heavy burden for the millions of victims and becomes a heavy burden for those who take their part."[58] The martyrs show us the heavy-ness of this very real burden. But the reality of the martyrs does not lie in some mystical identification with Christ. Instead, martyrdom comes as a result of following Christ. Sobrino sees the martyrs as examples of men and women who follow the command to take up the cross most literally. The martyrs' suffering and death come as a result of struggling against injustice, sometimes a systemic injustice. The martyrs encourage all Christians to take up the burden of reality in the cross, and in doing so provide the church a great service. Sobrino will argue that taking on the cross brings renewed credibility to the church. It evidences following Christ in a concrete manner. In this way we become a "church of Jesus."[59] The Jesus martyrs lead us to bear the burden of reality, to *"hacernos cargo de nuestra realidad,"* confirming that a greater love is possible by following Jesus and taking up the Cross.

The resurrection of Jesus forms the final piece of Sobrino's appeal. Sobrino claims that the martyrs invite us to share in Jesus's resurrection. While our sinful reality causes us to take on many burdens, the martyrs show us that we may also find grace in this reality. Sobrino is careful to point out that our reality is also impregnated with love and truth. The resurrection should then also be a reality in our lives. The martyrs help us to remember our freedom and our hope in the resurrection. He writes, "Living with hope against resignation, so that the mystery of iniquity, the not-yet, the certainly-not, and disappointment do not bury the promise . . . In this freedom, joy, and hope there is already a sort of reverberation of resurrection. This is the invitation the martyrs offer the church. And on all accounts their final appeal is not to forget them."[60] Christians can live as resurrected beings in part, because of the hope and freedom which the martyrs instill. As Kevin Burke and other theologians have asserted, the memory of the martyrs is very important. It heightens the imagination, and similar to the first Christian martyrs, becomes a seed for the faith.[61] As J. B. Metz asserts in his idea of the dangerous memory of Jesus, so too does the memory of the martyrs become dangerous: As the case studies in the fourth chapter will show, sometimes simply invoking the name of those who oppose the government or those forces which enable the anti-Kingdom, **is** inherently dangerous. These four appeals of Sobrino show the importance of the link between the Jesus martyrs and the crucified peoples: Jesus martyrs "have not concealed the face of God but have revealed it through their lives and deaths."[62] An attitude of gratitude surrounds the sacrifice of these martyrs. The martyrs, affected by the call of the crucified peoples, moved to model the cross of Jesus more intimately than most people, instill an even greater hope to remove the crucified peoples from their crosses.

The history and tradition of the martyrs is not sufficient to encapsulate all of the nuances for the martyrs of today. By rethinking the definition of martyrdom, Sobrino suggests the possibility of a new definition, and even the possibility of an anonymous martyr. But what is at the root of this thought? One might suggest that in order to understand why Sobrino wants to expand this definition, one must understand the Latin American experience which serves as his font. The next chapter examines the Latin American context in general, and the situation in El Salvador in particular which shapes not only the thought of Jon Sobrino but also explores the reality of martyrdom today.

NOTES

1. Blessed Father Miguel Pro, SJ died at the hands of a firing squad in northern Mexico in 1927. His famous words were *"Viva Cristo Rey"* or "Long Live Christ the King." He was executed after he continued to celebrate mass and the sacraments in spite of the government edict prohibiting all Church activities. His death coincides with the famous Mexican church movement, *Los Cristeros*, loosely translated "The Christ bearers." For an interesting literary link with Graham Greene's novel The Power and the Glory see Cunningham's *A Brief History of Saints*, pages 108–9.

2. *A Brief History of Saints*, 115.

3. Ibid, 116. Latin America is not the only example cited by Cunningham. He also mentions Northern Ireland, Yugoslavia, and the cases of Edith Stein and Dietrich Bonhoeffer.

4. Ibid, 116.

5. Cunningham, Lawrence. *"Causa Non Poena: On the Contemporary Martyrs."* In *More Than a Memory: The Discourse of Martyrdom and the Construction of Christian Identity in the History of Christianity*, ed. Johan Leemans, 451–64. Dudley, MA: Peeters, 2005, 454. Rahner's challenge will be examined more fully in the next section.

6. *Ut Unum Sint*, Paragraph number 84.

7. *A Brief History of Saints*, 118.

8. For more on this discussion see *A Brief History of Saints*, 122.

9. Ibid, 142. This question of the post-modern martyr is also an interesting one, but too involved to be treated sufficiently in this book.

10. *Novo Millennio Ineunte*, 41.

11. Metz, Johann Baptist and Schillebeeckx, Edward, ed. *Martyrdom Today*, Concilium. New York: The Seabury Press, 1983, 9.

12. *Martyrdom Today*, 10.

13. One only needs to think about the sack of Constantinople during the Crusades to find examples of soldiers who may have thought they were dying for the faith, when in truth they were killing Orthodox Christians. Ironically the Orthodox have a stronger case for martyrdom here!

14. *Martyrdom Today*, 10.

15. Ibid.

16. One could ask if Rahner is offering a parallel to the idea of the anonymous Christian. Is Rahner proposing the category of an anonymous martyr? He never states this explicitly, nor is he able to expand on the idea since he died the year after this essay was published.

17. With some exceptions, as Sobrino shows with his understanding of Jesus as proto-martyr.

18. A confessor is usually defined in the Roman Catholic church as one who suffers persecution and torture for the faith but not to the point of martyrdom.

19. *Martyrdom Today*, 10.

20. Rahner refers here to Thomas' Commentary on the Sentences, specifically in IV Sent. Dist. 49 q. 5 a.3. quaest. 2 ad, *Martyrdom Today*, 11.

21. Ibid, 13.
22. Ibid.
23. Ibid, 14.
24. Ibid.
25. Ibid, 19.
26. Ibid, 20.
27. Ibid, 22.
28. Ibid, 23. He quotes from Romero's homily on July 15, 1979.
29. Okure, Sobrino, and Wilfred, ed. *Rethinking Martyrdom*, Concilium. London: SCM Press, 2003, 7.
30. *Rethinking Martyrdom*, 7.
31. Ibid, 10.
32. Ibid, 16.
33. Ibid, 17.
34. Ibid. Italics author's emphasis.
35. Ibid, 18.
36. Ibid.
37. Ibid, 19.
38. Ibid, 20. Italics author's emphasis. Juan Luis Segundo argues that these poor are the church, but I will let this distinction go unchallenged here.
39. Ibid, 20.
40. Ibid.
41. Ibid, 21.
42. Ibid, 22. Italics author's emphasis.
43. Ibid, 23.
44. Ibid.
45. Ibid.
46. Ibid, 140.
47. Ibid, 140.
48. Ibid.
49. Ibid, 141.
50. Ibid.
51. Ibid, 140. Italics author's emphasis.
52. Ibid, 141. Italics author's emphasis.
53. Ibid, 142.
54. Ibid, 142. Brackets are my addition.
55. Ibid, 143. Italics author's emphasis.
56. Ibid. Italics author's emphasis.
57. Ibid, 143.
58. Ibid, 145. This idea of taking on the burden of reality comes from Ellacuría's "*hacerse cargo de la realidad.*" Kevin Burke discusses the extensive implications of this burden in *The Ground beneath the Cross: The Theology of Ignacio Ellacuria*. Washington D.C. : Georgetown University Press, 2000.
59. Ibid, 146.
60. Ibid, 148.

61. In a lecture commemorating the 25th anniversary of the "martyrs of the UCA" Kevin Burke highlighted the importance of this memory today. Marquette University Colloquium on the Martyrs of the UCA, November 2014.

62. Ibid.

Chapter Three

The Reality of Martyrdom in Latin America/El Salvador

INTRODUCTION

These next chapters provide a brief look at the larger Latin American context, showing how the political climate affected the church and the meaning of martyrdom. Next, I focus on the situation in Central America, particularly in El Salvador, with four exemplary cases of martyrdom there. The goal is to set the stage for understanding the significance of martyrdom in Latin American. The particular exemplary cases were chosen because they also have relevance in the life and theological work of Jon Sobrino.[1] These examples show us why Sobrino makes the claim for an expanded definition in as much as martyrdom is a reality which needs to be explored in its particularity and its depth and in light of its recent history.

THE LATIN AMERICAN REALITY: TWENTIETH CENTURY AND TODAY

The Latin American reality is complex both on the political and ecclesial levels. At a recent conference at Georgetown, presentations showed both how the church has contributed to as well as acted as a voice for democracy.[2] During the twentieth century in Latin America many historical changes take place which give rise to a central theme: the conflict between church and state. Before tackling the recent twentieth century history, a short disclaimer is necessary. Admittedly, the Catholic Church has a checkered history in Latin America, from the conquest of the Americas in the time of Columbus, to officially siding with the slave owners in the time of Bartolomé de Las Casas in the sixteenth century. One could write an entire book about the conquest of the Americas, or the history of Bartolomé de Las Casas.³ But while many priests came from Europe to the new world and blessed the imperial ways of their European sovereigns, there were also examples of prophetic voices. Las Casas, the Jesuit provincials who founded the reductions in South America, Saint Peter Claver, and Blessed Miguel Pro, all showed the ability to stand up and fight for the cause of justice.

In the twentieth century one can find examples of priests and bishops who stand up for the poor, and in particular the worker, as countries begin to industrialize. Catholic Action played a major role in setting up a dynamic of both cooperation and tension in many Latin American countries. Alberto Hurtado, SJ, a member of Catholic Action, founded a program of social service in Chile, *Hogar de Cristo*.⁴ This organization would later connect with the founder of the *Fe y Alegría* schools and basic housing projects like *Un Techo para Chile*, which today are found in most Latin American countries, but are especially strong in South America. However, in forming Catholic leaders Catholic Action also ran into trouble with many governments. State and federal governing bodies were not always open to receiving criticism from ecclesial bodies, regarding education, unions, and rights for all peoples. These conflicts were not exclusive to South America but were found in Central America and Mexico as well.

Before describing the historical and political situation in El Salvador it is necessary to mention those countries which provide important elements of the larger background history of Latin America. In the past century, Mexico provides one example of a contentious relationship between the church and the government. The well documented history of the *Cristeros* rebellion and Miguel Pro, SJ exemplify a time in the twentieth century when the Mexican government did not support church activities. In fact, many church leaders were killed for opposing the government, or simply for celebrating Mass or praying in church. Robert Royal recounts, "Countless other priests met terrible ends: shot in their vestments during Mass, thrown from trains, executed and dragged behind vehicles, tortured for information, 'disappeared'—a term that would commonly be used decades later for similar cases all over Latin America."⁵ One of the principal figures of this time period was Miguel Pro, SJ who despite many obstacles returned to his country from Europe in order to serve the many Catholics who were suffering repression. In order to minister as a priest, he disguised himself to blend in with his surroundings and avoid arrest by the state and local police. Royal notes, "Photographs from this time period show him in various disguises . . . When it was a women's association, he dressed in a stylish suit and straw boater. For the workingmen, he put on overalls and a worker's cap; he looked like a fellow driver for a meeting of chauffeurs, a mechanic among mechanics. By various subterfuges he was able to hear confessions even in jails."⁶ In the end Pro's great ministerial successes would lead to his downfall. Under the pretext that they were aiding an assassination attempt, Miguel and two of his brothers were arrested and thrown in prison. Miguel Pro walked bravely to his execution, and asked to pray before dying. Royal relates, "After a few minutes, he stood up, extended his arms in the form of a cross, a traditional Mexican posture in prayer, and with a steady voice, neither defiant nor desperate, movingly intoned words that have since become famous, 'Viva Cristo Rey,' 'Long Live Christ the King.'"⁷ To date, Miguel Pro has only been beatified and not officially named a martyr for the faith. But popularly he is accepted by many as a martyr in his native Mexico and elsewhere. He fits into the same problematic of categorization that the church has with naming those martyrs who died for political reasons in predominantly Christian countries.

SOUTH AMERICA: BRAZIL AND ARGENTINA

In the 1950s and 1960s many Catholic groups in Latin America found themselves in the line of fire. When members of Catholic Action organized they often protested the conditions of many workers. These organizations were not well received in the cold war period, and many were branded Communists. Also increasing in frequency throughout Latin America, many repressive governments targeted church leaders. Following the repression of the *Cristero* movement in Mexico, the 1950s and 1960s abound with stories from a number of different countries. During this time period in South America, the repression occurred first in Brazil and Argentina. In the case of Brazil, Dom Helder Câmara serves as an exemplary model for a bishop, predating Archbishop Romero in El Salvador.

Gustavo Gutiérrez remarks that the repression in Brazil began long before the conflicts in most Spanish speaking countries in Latin America.⁸ The conflict in Brazil began in 1968 and lasted until 1979. Some scholars claim the conflict came about because of the differing traditions which existed in Brazil at the time, a kind of "Church of Two Christendoms."⁹ Over time the official church position changed from a conservative and static one to see a more progressive church with a voice for the voiceless, a voice for the poor. This sparked conflicts, especially when wealthier parishes representing the status quo clashed with Christian base communities (CEB). Some of these disputes were not easily resolved and led to the targeting of priests and religious by some para-military forces who used brute force. One priest in northern Brazil was tortured, killed and then dragged by a jeep through a small town to serve as an example for what happened to those who sided with the poor.¹⁰ The list of martyrs in Brazil continues to accumulate even today. Sister Dorothy Stang is perhaps the most recent example of someone who died for her faith, due to her defense of land rights of indigenous peoples and farmers in the Amazon Rain Forest.[11]

During the 1970s, the Republic of Argentina experienced a period of political violence which continued until a constitutional government was established in 1983, the so-called "Dirty War." While the violence perhaps never escalated into a full civil war, the armed forces did overthrow the constitutional government in March of 1976.[12] When the coup occurred, some of the bishops sided with the military, most noticeably the bishop of Paraná, but also the Vicar of the Armed Forces, Monsignor Adolfo Tortolo. He could not have been unaware of the repressive methods the armed forces decided to use. Anyone associated with the progressive youth group Acción Catolica (Catholic Action) was in grave peril. More than 4,000 people were "disappeared," likely tortured and then killed, their bodies never found. Among them were two French nuns, Sisters Alice Domón and Léonie Duquet. Emilio Mignon writes, "The bodies of those assassinated were thrown out of planes belonging to the armed forces into the Plata River and the Atlantic Ocean."[13] During the clandestine repression many of the military bishops and chaplains "publicly and privately justified the torture, assassinations and abuses by the armed forces exempting its members from moral responsibility. They even developed a supposed doctrine with that meaning."[14]

Some Argentinian bishops did side with human rights groups at the time, and the bishop of La Rioja, Enrique Angelelli, was killed by the armed forces in a simulated traffic accident August 4, 1976.[15] The Vatican was well aware of the persecution and John Paul II referred to the disappearances on three separate occasions.[16] The Argentine cardinals and bishops tried to scale down and reinterpret his allocutions. In the end, two bishops, sixteen priests, and a number of brothers, nuns, and seminarians were killed.[17] The excuse used for the killing of most of the priests and religious was that they had identified too literally with the Gospel. One naval Admiral purportedly remarked to a priest, "Your mistake is having interpreted too literally Christ's doctrine. Christ speaks for the poor, but it is the poor in spirit and you have gone to live with the poor. In Argentina, the poor in spirit are the rich, who are those who are spiritually in need."[18]

Chile

Besides the entry of grapes and wines into the U.S. markets, Chile is perhaps most known for Augusto Pinochet's long dictatorship which lasted from 1973 to 1990. But the relationship between the church and the state began to change much earlier, in part due to the influence of Catholic Social Action groups and political leaders. In Chile, when a known socialist, Allende, took office, the U.S. backed Pinochet regime staged a coup. Leading up to 1973, the era of Christian Democrats with the first President Frei, there were a number of different approaches to the conflicts between labor leaders and business owners, between agrarian reforms and large landowners and the growing social concern for the great disparities between rich and poor.[19] Many Christian base ecclesial communities were formed during this period, and usually contained a component of social justice.[20] As the 1970s approached, the church remained neutral in the upcoming political elections. Cardinal Silva "declared that the Church favored no party or candidate, and that clerics should not publicly support any political ideology or movement."[21] When Salvador Allende won the popular vote, a plurality of only 36.2 percent, support of Catholics in Santiago jumped from 10 to 22 percent. The relationship with the church and Allende's government later deteriorated over the program of social humanism in all schools, public and private, but while the relations were strained they never completely broke down.[22]

The Catholic church's reaction to the military coup in 1973 was a mixture of concern and relief. Because of this cautious support of Pinochet's regime the church was allowed to set up coup emergency relief programs for foreign refugees and Chileans suffering from the repression.[23] The social service arm, COPACHI, became the most reliable source for information on what was happening throughout the country and its reports would later attest to the human rights violations. Archbishop Silva of Santiago would later found the *Vicaría de la Solidaridad* in 1976.[24] The church however did remain divided. In 1975 three fifths of the bishops interviewed did not support liberation theology, and most of those supported the Pinochet regime. Many priests and local leaders thought otherwise, however. Almost 50 percent of all priests and nuns disagreed with the government policies and practices, and many were trying to combine their work in the CEBs with a critical reflection on church social teachings and political problems. Brian Smith concludes that "The Chilean Church has significantly shifted the fulcrum point of its strategy of relating to society and fulfilling its religious mission over the past half-century. It has definitely rejected the traditional Christendom approach, and in so doing no longer identifies so closely with the interests of State nor of upper-class groups."[25] In Chile today, now more than twenty five years after the dictatorship, major work on reconciliation must still take place to heal the vast divisions within the Catholic Church.

The Catholic Church in Chile can be criticized on a number of fronts for its actions in the dictatorships. For those with more progressive politics, the hierarchy and church leaders did not respond quickly enough to the repression of a purportedly Roman Catholic government. For Pinochet, who considered himself a faithful Catholic and even went to daily Mass, some church elements were aligning themselves with Leftist politicians, and in his opinion the church hierarchy needed to control its members. Priests became targets, just as lay ministers of CEBs were targeted and other church leaders were simply rounded up along with other Communists or Socialist party members. They joined the ranks of the disappeared. Lay leaders in Pudahuel at the *Capilla Jesús Vida Nueva* still speak about the roundups. Some mothers never saw their children again. Men and women in the community simply joined the ranks of the *desaparecidos*, the disappeared.[26]

Even such a brief overview as provided here shows that a history of violence and political unrest is not limited to Central America and El Salvador. I realize that the examples used above are not exhaustive, and many other examples of political strife, martyrs and the disappeared could be drawn from many different countries. In fact, almost all of Latin America has been affected at some point. This context of violence and unrest sets the stage for discussing what it means to be a Latin American martyr. As we saw in chapter one, Sobrino and others make the claim for an expanded definition of martyrdom, a definition rooted in Latin American reality.

El Salvador

While South America endured forceful dictatorships and strong tensions between church and state, the social strife in Central America led to an even greater problematic, that of civil war. While Chile, Brazil, Argentina and other countries experienced violence and conflict included the military and heavy arms buildup, Guatemala, Nicaragua, and finally El Salvador would experience hand to hand combat in the streets, armed conflict, and especially in the case of El Salvador, civil war. While we focus our attention on El Salvador as the setting for the context of Jon Sobrino's Christology and ideas concerning martyrdom, Guatemala and Nicaragua also warrant further study. Much of the violence in these countries erupted due to similar social problems. Since El Salvador most directly relates to the four selected case studies, the focus will be on this small Central American country.

As one might expect the military conflict in El Salvador affected all sectors of the population. In the ecclesial sphere, much occurred in El Salvador between 1977 and 1989. The death of Rutilio Grande in 1977, the assassination of Archbishop Romero, the deaths of the U.S. nuns and laywoman, Ita Ford, Maura Clarke, Dorothy Kazel, Jean Donovan in 1980, and the murders of the Jesuits on the lawn outside their community in 1989, all serve as examples of martyrs in this checkered history. These exemplary martyrs are highlighted but there were many others also killed at this time. Not to be forgotten are the thousands of everyday people also lost their lives, in addition to the lay catechists, Salvadoran and missionary priests, brothers, and women religious who were also killed.

These particular martyrs were chosen as examples because of their impact in El Salvador and internationally. The argument begins with Rutilio Grande because of the effect his death had on the Salvadoran church, and the fact that he was the first native Salvadoran priest killed for political reasons in the 1970s. His death coincides with the start of Oscar Romero's appointment as archbishop. At Grande's funeral Romero preached a long homily against the violence perpetrated in the rural areas of El Salvador.[27] Next, we must consider the extensive impact of Romero's short tenure as archbishop, and the impact, both national and international of his death on civil war, politics and church life in El Salvador. The four U.S. churchwomen also receive important mention. While perhaps nationwide in El Salvador they do not enjoy the same reverence as the other martyrs, their deaths did make a tremendous impact, especially because their deaths brought attention to the civil war in El Salvador in the United States and internationally. Finally, we will see the impact of the deaths of the Jesuit martyrs in 1989. This event can be seen as a bookend to Romero's death, in that it marks the beginning of the end of the war. Local and international outcry was strong, especially since five of the six priests killed were Spanish citizens. The international outcry helped bring about the end of the war. All of these martyrs shape the sense of what it means to be a martyr in the twentieth century.

NOTES

1. In fact, if you visit Sobrino's office at the UCA there are three photos on the wall across from his desk, Rutilio Grande, Oscar Romero, and Ignacio Ellacuría.

2. See Matt Carnes and John Thiede's presentation on politics and democracy in Latin America at Georgetown's Berkeley Center and its forthcoming publication.

3. For example, Gutiérrez, Gustavo. *Las Casas: In Search of the Poor of Jesus Christ*. Translated by Robert R. Barr. Eugene, Oregon: Wipf and Stock Publishers, 1995. For a missionary history see Helen Rand Parrish's edited book on Las Casas, especially the introduction to the book: Las Casas, Bartolomé de. *The Only Way*. Translated by Francis Patrick Sullivan, SJ ed. Helen Rand Parish. New York: Paulist Press, 1992.

4. For more on Catholic Action see the introduction to Royal, Robert. *The Catholic Martyrs of the Twentieth Century*. New York: The Crossroad Publishing Company, 2000. Alberto Hurtado, SJ was canonized a saint by the Catholic Church. He died in 1952 but founded many works. *Hogar de Cristo* and *Techo para Chile* are now very strong social service organizations serving as soup kitchens, shelters, and house building projects for the poor. *Fe y Alegría* schools first founded for the rural poor in Venezuela and Columbia, now form a network of schools throughout Latin America

and can now be found in poor urban areas as well, Santiago de Chile serving as only one example. Rough translations as follows: *Hogar de Cristo* = home of Christ; *Techo para Chile* = A Roof for Chile; *Fe y Alegría* = Faith and Joy. For a great collection of the life and writings of St. Alberto Hurtado see *Escritos de San Alberto Hurtado* published by the *Centro de Estudios San Alberto Hurtado* in the Pontificia Universidad Catolica de Chile, Santiago, 2007.

5. Royal, Robert. *The Catholic Martyrs of the Twentieth Century*. New York: The Crossroad Publishing Company, 2000, 33. This term "disappeared" while perhaps coined during the time of Miguel Pro, was made common throughout the horrible history of violence in Latin America. Thousands of people were "disappeared" in the various dictatorships, especially in Brazil, Argentina and Chile. Pinochet's regime had a plan to make any political opposition leaders "disappear." Foreign nationals were most often deported, but others were buried in mass graves, or bodies were simply dumped off the ocean shores, often after long torture sessions. William Cavanaugh speaks of the effects of this treatment in his book, *Torture and the Eucharist*: Challenges in Contemporary Theology, ed. Gareth Jones and Louis Ayres. Oxford: Blackwell Publishers, 1998.

6. *The Catholic Martyrs*, 35.

7. Ibid, 18.

8. Interview with Gustavo Gutiérrez, November, 2008.

9. Keogh, Dermot, ed. *Church and Politics in Latin America*. New York: St. Martin's Press, 1990, 301. See pages 300 to the end of the book for an interesting description of church and politics.

10. Interview with Gustavo Gutiérrez, November, 2008.

11. See Murphy, Roseanne. *Martyr of the Amazon: The Life of Sister Dorothy Stang*. New York: Orbis Books, 2007 or Le Breton, Binka. *The Greatest Gift: The Courageous Life and Martyrdom of Sister Dorothy Stang*. New York: Doubleday, 2007. For a concise connection between martyrdom and her life see Thiede, John S. "Martyrdom and the Good of Creation: The Case of Dorothy Stang." *God, Grace & Creation*. College Theology Society Annual Volume 55 (2009): 252–63.

12. Keogh, Dermot, ed. *Church and Politics in Latin America*. New York: St. Martin's Press, 1990, 356.

13. Ibid. Jesuits in Chile tell a similar story of looking out from the Jesuit community house in Las Brisas and seeing bodies dropped out of helicopters during the Pinochet years.

14. Ibid, 358.

15. Ibid. Gustavo Gutiérrez also remarks that the killing of Angelelli was significant. For many years the Argentinian military denied any involvement, but today both U.S. and Argentine military documents show that he was a target of elite special forces and right wing paramilitary groups. Interview, October 2009.

16. Ibid, 364.

17. Ibid, 367.

18. Ibid, 369.

19. I note that this was the first President Frei, because his son would also later become President.

20. Christian Base Communities, Base Ecclesial Communities, or "Communidades de Base." From here forward I abbreviate them as CEBs.

21. *Church and Politics in Latin America*, 324.

22. Ibid, 327.

23. Ibid, 329. The Church arm was later named COPACHI or the Committee of Co-Operation for Peace. This would be established in 22 of 25 provinces, and lend legal aid service to prisoners or those unemployed because of their associations with the Allende's government.

24. Ibid, 16. Translation = Vicariate of Solidarity.

25. Ibid, 338. Though from personal experience this still is an issue today. The church of the poor and the upper class can appear quite different, and wealthier parishes might have two or three priests while poorer parishes might have one priest who serves four or five "*capillas*," small churches or chapels with over 10,000 families. The ratio 3:10,000 vs. 1: 50,000 is telling.

26. Interview with pastoral team of *Capilla Jesús Vida Nueva* in Pudahuel, Chile, January 2009.

27. Cavada, Miguel, ed. *Homilias: Monsenor Oscar A. Romero*. Vol. 1. San Salvador, El Salvador: UCA Editores, 2005, 31–36.

Chapter Four

Four Examplars

Rutilio Grande, Archbishop Romero, U.S. Churchwomen, UCA Martyrs

RUTILIO GRANDE

It is necessary to introduce these martyrs in their chronological order rather than trying to assign some type of historical or theological weight to their deaths. While some might start the story of the war in El Salvador with the assassination of Archbishop Oscar Romero, they would be mistaken. U.N. Truth commission documents, Anna Peterson, and Phillip Berryman all date the war from 1980 to 1992, not coincidentally the year Reagan began his presidency. The violence and indications of war arguably broke out five years earlier. The military organized harsh responses to any form of community organizing or the formation of unions in the coffee, sugar cane, and fruit export regions. In terms of the conflict between the paramilitary forces and church lay catechists and leaders, these church men and women began to be killed as early as 1976. Thus, Rutilio Grande, SJ is important not only as a potential martyr, but also in the history of El Salvador. First, he was one of the first Jesuit priests to be threatened with death, was a target of paramilitary groups and was eventually killed. Second, his death caused church authorities to further investigate what was happening in the "*campo*," or the countryside, in the far reaches of El Salvador. Finally, there is a direct link between the death of Rutilio Grande, Romero and the Jesuits killed in 1989. One could argue that the murder of Rutilio Grande started an ugly chapter in church history in El Salvador. While that chapter begins with his death, his life is also worth describing and celebrating.

Rutilio Grande was born July 5, 1928, in the village of El Paisnal, in El Salvador. His father was an important small business person and was politically important in the town. He lived a fairly normal life, and was especially close to his godfather Vicente Tejada, who would later help support his seminary studies. He was also close to another "padrino" Facundo Barrera, in whose home the visiting priests stayed.[1] In this house young Rutilio probably met the future Archbishop of San Salvador, Monseñor Luis Chávez, with whom he maintained a close correspondence even after he became a Jesuit. When Rutilio was only twelve, he wrote to the Archbishop for the first time telling him about his desire to become a priest. After he completed elementary school, Rutilio entered the minor seminary, and finished high school there. During his studies for his bachelor's degree he felt called to enter the Society of Jesus, and with the approval of the archbishop, he entered the novitiate on September 23, 1945.[2]

Rutilio Grande completed two years of the novitiate when he was 19, and took vows in Los Chorros, Venezuela on September 24, 1947. He studied science and humanities in Quito, Ecuador, but due to health issues interrupted his studies to work for a while in Central America. He taught for a year at Colegio Javier, the Jesuit high school in Panama. Afterward, he was transferred to the seminary in San Salvador, where he was a professor of Latin, Spanish, Geography and History. In 1953, he was sent to philosophy studies in Oña, Spain where he received his licentiate in 1956. In October, he went straight to theology studies and was ordained a priest on July 30, 1959. He said his first mass in Oña, and some Salvadoran families were present including the *Consúl* who brought a Salvadoran flag which was placed next to the altar. Father Grande had planned for a fourth year of theology in the United States, but due to health reasons he had to remain in Spain.[3] In August of 1962, he finished his Jesuit formation in the tertianship program in Córdoba, Spain. Afterward, in a brief period of special studies in Brussels, at the International Pastoral Institute *Lumen Vitae*, he developed an initial pastoral action plan, which he would later utilize more when he returned to pastoral work in Aguilares.[4] As Thomas M. Kelly acknowledges, this pastoral formation was something Rutilio learned and the Latin American Bishops Conference (CELAM) at Medellín prescribed a similar approach. This pastoral method of see, judge and act were essential to Grande's adoption of a rural pastoral plan.[5] But instead of going into pastoral work after his final vows in Brussels, on August 15, 1964, he was missioned to teach at the Seminary in San Salvador.[6]

The return to work at the seminary, this time as a fully formed Jesuit priest, proved bittersweet. On the one hand, the return to El Salvador must have been welcome. But returning with new ideas from Belgium and in the wake of a Second Vatican Council which would take longer to be received in El Salvador, Padre "Tilo" would be hurt by some of his interactions with the local hierarchy and some of the more conservative seminary staff.[7] Rutilio himself would describe it as a theological crisis between a pre-conciliar theology and new ideas from the Council like the common priesthood of the people of God.

Some of his ideas, formulated during his studies in Belgium, also conflicted with the local archbishop's pastoral plan for the poor.[8] Rutilio advocated a change, and vocally supported more work with the poor for the seminarians. He cited the ideas of Paul VI in *Populorum Progressio* especially emphasizing the scandal when a very few enjoy all of the goods, but while he proved a student favorite, others both inside the seminary and in the oligarchy accused him of a "reheated Marxism."[9] In the end, Tilo would ask for a change of ministry from his Jesuit superiors, and would eventually resign from his duties in the seminary when he felt he had lost the confidence of the bishops.[10]

The change of ministries allowed Rutilio to take a short sabbatical. He went to the Institute for Latin American Pastoral Work in Ecuador for some studies, and was also allowed a trip to visit the grave of his deceased Salesian brother, who had served as a priest in Costa Rica. Rutilio was in Europe when his brother died in 1964, and was unable to return for the funeral or visit the grave site in Costa Rica before this time. In 1972, Grande was missioned by his provincial to head the new area of pastoral ministry for the Central American province. He had many new ideas for this ministry, starting with his training in Belgium, continuing in his pastoral work in the countryside while teaching at the seminary, and finally crystallizing during his time at the pastoral institute in Ecuador.[11] He wrote to the Vice Provincial asserting that the primary and fundamental option for this work should be: "a pastoral work in teams, in a rural zone of peasants or a marginalized semi-urban zone oriented to an integral promotion (of values) based in a Christian consciousness."[12] Rutilio imagined that he and his Jesuit brothers were the ideal group to carry out this plan. He envisioned an agile group, a team which could set up an apostolic mission in a remote area and not be restricted by outside constraints. He hoped that their pastoral plan would fit the difficult reality of the great majority living in El Salvador at the time. Thomas Kelly notes, "Rutilio decided to form a team of Jesuits to begin an experiment in rural evangelization that would change the face of pastoral work in El Salvador. What he embarked on could aptly be termed 'immersion pastoral activity.'"[13] This immersed pastoral activity produced almost immediate success. Within a few months almost 32 CEBs were functioning and local leaders soon became agents in their own development.[14]

Upon Rutilio Grande's arrival in Aguilares in early 1973 his pastoral plan met with resistance from the wealthy landowners, and the families representing the oligarchy in San Salvador at the time. But his time in Aguilares, just before the beginning of the civil war, was greeted with great rejoicing among the people there. In some ways, this was the story of the prodigal son returning home after many years away. While he had visited home many times while at the seminary, it was the first time in his Jesuit life he had worked full time in the area where he had grown up. But while Rutilio saw himself as a servant of all and wanted to find ways of liberating the people both spiritually and economically, he was branded as a "communist priest."[15] One photo from a rally on the feast of Corpus Christi in Aguilares shows a group of *campesinos* holding a sign which says, "Jesus is with us when we denounce the injustices."[16] The powers that be, most of whom were practicing Catholics, couldn't have appreciated the thought that Jesus was on the side of their coffee pickers and the rural work force in general.

Before coming to Aguilares, Grande had made his eight day annual retreat at Santa Tecla with at least one Jesuit who would be a member of his pastoral team. Here, Grande replanted the idea of the first and fundamental option for pastoral ministry. He decided on a method which was personalized, "dialogal," and rooted in a sphere of "action-reflection-action."[17] Rutilio hoped that the method's fundamental base would be found in the Gospel, and in making that Gospel accessible and relevant to the campesinos who lived in Aguilares and the surrounding countryside. When Rutilio arrived at the parish in September 1972, he found that most of the local economy was sustained by the growth of sugar cane. But the majority of the people living there, over 90 percent had only 22 percent of the available land to farm, and that only 140 days of the year.[18] Most of the large "*haciendas*," the name for the largest privately owned farms with sugar cane, coffee, and cotton, were geared toward export. In the years before Grande arrived, conditions were worsening for the majority of the people, as small farmers were manipulated or pushed out by the larger haciendas. As a result, many people were malnourished or even starving.[19] Rutilio took great exception to the fact that more and more products were being exported, while Salvadoran citizens were dying of hunger, or malnourishment.

Rutilio Grande ministered in an area which contained a small town Aguilares, with 10,000 inhabitants, a small village El Paisnal, with 2,000 inhabitants, and a large rural sector of 170 square kilometers (102 sq. miles) where 18,000 people lived on or near thirty-five large haciendas.[20] Rutilio saw in this rural land a major problem of exploitation. The large landowners and some town politicians and local police lived fairly comfortably, while the large majority struggled to make a living wage. Rutilio saw first-hand the effects which were denounced in papal documents as early as *Populorum Progressio* and which he himself denounces in a short article in 1970.[21] He argues that the social sphere is also a church sphere, and cites Leo XIII, Pius X, Pius XI, and Paul VI, especially the idea that the right to private property cannot outweigh the common good. In fact, papal teaching sides with the common good and limits private ownership of property when it promotes inequality, or injustice. Rutilio and his pastoral team "entered the explosive and conflictive area just at the moment in Salvadoran Society when the contradictions were becoming even more sharp."[22] But the great irony was that they were not implementing anything which conflicted with papal teachings or the recent statements from Latin American bishops. As Kelly remarks, "Far from being merely activists these leaders were faithful and orthodox Catholics. It is also important to note that the work of both priests was fully supported by the Latin American bishops. Creating peasant organizations, building faith communities relevant to the context, and advocating for land reform were all *specific* topics advocated in the practical sections of the conference's concluding documents."[23]

The pastoral team's first task was to attempt to create space for the nourishment and spiritual growth of the Catholic community in the area. The pastoral team divided the town and village into ten mission centers, and the country into fifteen mission centers. They created base ecclesial communities in each area, and formed local leaders to be responsible for liturgies and pastoral councils. Rutilio's preaching also became sharper as he delved deeper into the lives of the people and listened to their stories of despair and injustice. He became known for the explosiveness and passion in his preaching. When preaching once on the Magnificat he praised Mary as an example of a beautiful yet typical woman. He went on to say, that she "was the opposite from all of those who live in the center of the wasp's nest, who have bought votes . . . those who celebrate over there in the Sheraton hotel."[24] In his homily he spoke out against the political corruption, and the exorbitant expense of hosting the Miss Universe pageant in the Hotel Sheraton when people were dying of hunger. When the pastoral team confronted the unjust social structures in and around Aguilares, they were denounced, and farm workers were warned not to organize into cooperatives or unions. Rutilio utilized an idea that also would appear in Sobrino's 1976 book, *Cristología desde Latinoamérica*. He preached about being in the midst of "a crisis in Galilee," just as Jesus was persecuted by the powerful, and the disciples failed to understand his teaching.[25] Through this prophetic preaching, Rutilio became the most visible symbol of a religious movement that advocated not only a reform of the rural parishes, but also social change. From 1973 until his death, Rutilio lived through an internal struggle between the purity of his ideas and the harsh reality of life around him.

During this time, the political landscape in the country grew more and more conflictive. Other groups came into the area to organize the campesinos.[26] When accusations arose tying his pastoral work to Marxist influences, Grande traveled to the capital to speak with both the President and Archbishop Chávez about the accusations. He made the argument that everything that they were doing was in line with the Gospels and the papal teachings and claimed that his only political affiliation was to the common good of the great majority of people in the area.[27] But the good relationship with the President would not last long. In May of 1975, President Molina claimed that there were "communist priests" in the area, and Father Rafael Palacios, a diocesan priest who worked in the parish next to Grande's, was severely beaten that month.[28]

Rutilio Grande and his pastoral team were faced with three main alternatives: flee the area due to the conflict, look for a compromise solution with local politicians and opposition forces, or continue to grow the parish openly running the risk of conflict both in the parish and nationally. In the end, they made the decision to continue growing the parish, deciding that a good pastoral initiative must take on the risks. In the elections of 1977, General Romero won the presidency almost two to one, with allegations of fraud.[29] Archbishop Chávez helped mediate a solution where the opposition candidate and other party leaders could seek asylum and leave the country. The government initiated a concerted campaign against some priests, and some priests and religious were expelled from the country. Two ex-Jesuit students who had worked in Aguilares were expelled from the country, as were three priests from the parish next to Aguilares, Mario Bernal from Columbia, Guillaume Denaux, Belgium, and Bernardo Servil, North America.[30]

A mass protest was organized by the local Vicariate which ended in a Eucharist, and Rutilio Grande preached the homily which would eventually lead to his death. Soon after, authorities detained and tortured with electric shock a Spaniard, Juan José Ramirez, for ten days, not knowing he had left the Jesuit Order. Also, Archbishop Chávez resigned due to age, and Archbishop Romero took possession of the diocese in a private ceremony. Rutilio changed his tack, trying to emphasize how the parish goals were in line with that of the Republic, and he denounced human rights violations and injustice in the area. He tried to explain his position at all levels, to the new Archbishop, the Ministry of the Interior and even the President.[31] Grande asked the President to come to Aguilares to learn about the situation and publically stated he would dialog with anyone, even those who disagreed with him. In Rutilio's homily on February 13 in Apopa, he preached about a common humanity, and spoke out against the government's expulsion of Mario Bernal. Dramatically and tellingly, he claimed that "the hour of the martyr" had arrived, that the Gospel message was subversive, and that it was dangerous to be a Christian.[32]

Rutilio Grande began to see an increase in the fervency and number of personal death threats over the next month. Rumors circulated that even some of his own relatives were angry with him, and planning something against him. On Saturday March 12, barely one month after Apopa, Rutilio Grande, SJ joined the list of the martyrs in Latin America. He left to preside at the

Eucharist in El Paisnal, with Manuel Solórzano, 72, Nelson Rutilio Lemus, 16, and two or three children who accompanied him on the trip as they crossed the sugar cane fields.[33] They drove right into an ambush. The bullets which rained down on the vehicle came from the front, side, and even from behind.[34] Bullets entered Rutilio's neck at two different points, various bullets struck the lumbar region, others broke his pelvis. Twelve of his wounds were deemed mortal wounds by the coroner. When the bullets hit, Tilo lost control of the vehicle, and when it left the road it turned on its side with the motor still running, and the children in the back were able to escape the vehicle.[35] Don Manuel and Nelson Lemus were also dead at the scene.

News of the deaths was immediately sent to the Cathedral and the Jesuit Provincial. The deaths were officially reported as being caused by firearms. The Provincial asked that the three bodies be placed in identical coffins. The Provincial, three Jesuits, Archbishop Romero, and auxiliary Bishop Rivera all arrived that evening. The President promised an independent investigation, an investigation which to this day remains open, with no one charged in the deaths. Some suspect that there were many different parties responsible and some may still be living in the Aguilares area.[36] Many people came into the village when they heard of the news, and the church was overflowing at the vigil. The bodies were then transferred to the cathedral where the Jesuit provincial presided at the funeral mass, accompanied by the bishops and over 100 priests concelebrated. Both the provincial and Archbishop Romero gave stirring homilies. The cadavers were led in three hearses in procession back to El Paisnal for burial, with a long string of vehicles trailing behind. One participant would later write a song based on the experience whose refrain repeats: "Walking with Rutilio on the road to El Paisnal, like Christ walked his way to the Cross."[37]

The homily Archbishop Romero gave that day was perhaps his most stirring early homily. Perhaps since the provincial gave a more personalized homily about Rutilio's life, the new Archbishop chose to focus on the reality in El Salvador. He began by stating that if it were a simple funeral he would speak about the human and personal relations with Father Rutilio Grande to whom he felt as close as a brother. But Romero declared that the funeral was not a time to speak personally, rather a time to reflect on the significance of Rutilio's death. He cited Paul VI, and asked the question "What does the church offer in this universal fight for the liberation from all this misery?"[38] The liberation which the church offers is the same as Father Grande offered, a preaching filled with solidarity for the faith, and given to the joy of God, and a message which is in union with the Church. Romero claimed that Rutilio Grande, SJ died preaching the social doctrine of the faith, and this message would be of great importance for all who want to work together with the

Gospel message. He made a personal plea to those responsible for the murders, "I want to tell you, criminal brothers, who already are in ex-communion with the church, and are listening on the radio . . . I want to tell you, criminal brothers, that we love you and we ask God for forgiveness for your hearts, because the love of the church is not capable of hating, it does not have enemies. The love of the Lord inspired the action of Rutilio Grande."[39]

Clearly, Romero was affected by the death of Rutilio Grande, the first native Salvadoran priest to be murdered in the 1970s for political reasons. In fact, his homilies during 1979 are filled with references to Tilo. In one reference he thanked the Society of Jesus for assigning men like Rutilio to El Salvador, and "illuminating so many on the roads to Aguilares."[40] Jon Sobrino would later write an article calling Rutilio Grande the "proto-martyr" of El Salvador, referring to his death as the one that would signal the rupture between the Catholic Church and the state, and marking the start of the greatest conflict in El Salvador.[41] On a national level, Rutilio Grande is still remembered as a martyr for justice, and one can still find pictures of him in Aguilares, the capital of San Salvador, and as far north as Chalatenango. Sobrino is not alone in celebrating his martyrdom. Sobrino still looks at Rutilio Grande as one of his "brothers," and his picture hangs on the wall facing his desk, along with Oscar Romero and Ignacio Ellacuría.[42] Recently the cause for his beatification has also been opened.

ARCHBISHOP OSCAR ROMERO

Martin Maier, SJ claims that one can find many similarities between the life of Oscar Romero and Jesus of Nazareth. For the same reason Sobrino uses the life of Monseñor Romero as an example of a Jesuanic martyr. Maier categorizes the years between 1917 and 1943 as the path to presbyteral ordination for Oscar Arnulfo Romero. He was born August 15, 1917, the second of eight children, in Ciudad Barrios, a rural mountain city in the northeast of El Salvador, on the Honduran border.[43] His parents were both considered *mestizos* meaning that their blood lines were mixed with both native and Spanish blood. The main agricultural work in Ciudad Barrios was tied to coffee, and Romero's mother had a small piece of land which she used to cultivate coffee to help support the family. His father ran the telegraph in town, and his mother also helped with the mail. As a boy, Oscar was very devoted to the church, and would leave from morning mass to help his mother distribute the letters. He also learned how to play the flute and his nickname in town was "the flute boy."[44] Due to a childhood illness at age four, Oscar was undersized, and was known for his timid nature. After completing the third grade, he began an apprenticeship to be a carpenter, but showed little or no aptitude. He did, however, show great aptitude with all things spiritual and was known for his piety. At age 13, he went to the minor seminary in San Miguel, run by the Claretian Fathers. During this time, Oscar was always active in church, prayed often, and regularly read the *Imitation of Christ*, by Thomas a Kempis.[45]

In 1937, Romero transferred to the major seminary in San Salvador, run by the Jesuits. He was selected to go to Rome, in great part due to his rhetorical talent. Romero studied at the Gregorian University in Rome and made the Ignatian Spiritual Exercises for the first time.[46] He showed a special interest in spiritual theology, and was especially dedicated to St. Augustine, John of the Cross, and Teresa of Ávila. He was ordained to the priesthood on April 4, 1942. He began a doctoral thesis in Rome, but his bishop recalled him to El Salvador in 1943 before he could finish, in part because of World War II. During this period he wrote a short article about priesthood, in which he describes a priest as "being with Christ, a crucified person who redeems. To be with Christ is to be a resurrected person, who gives out resurrection and life."[47] Both Jesus Delgado and Maier note that many of Romero's ideals early in his priesthood revolved around the idea of a Christ crucified, a Christ who redeems, and a priest who lives a simple life of pastoral care.

After celebrating his first mass in Barrios, Romero became the pastor of the parish in San Miguel, where he served from 1944–1967. Here, Romero befriended both the poor and the rich. He was inspired by St. Vincent de Paul and lived by the following rule: "I collect donations from the rich to give to the poor. In this way, it alleviates the problems of the poor, and the consciences of the rich."[48] For many years, the church used this philosophy to justify and to help unjust social situations, not just in El Salvador. Later in his life, Romero would criticize this attitude, and distanced himself from it, especially as archbishop. Martin Maier thinks that for this reason, many biographers characterize him as a traditional priest, Delgado included. But Maier asserts that Romero also experienced a tension with his brother priests, in part because he was intolerant of their faults, but also because he had studied in Rome he had few friends in the local diocesan clergy. Soon enough this introverted priest would blossom in the national episcopacy and make many international contacts as well.

In 1967, rumors circulated that Romero would be made auxiliary bishop with the right of succession in his local diocese, but instead, he was "promoted" to San Salvador, and made secretary of the Episcopal Conference.[49] The goodbyes in San Miguel were very difficult for him, and it was not an easy departure. He wrote in the last bulletin, "Obedient to the service of the church, I must leave for San Salvador . . . from where I will continue to love and do the good that I can for San Miguel. . . ."⁵⁰ Monseñor Romero would live first in the seminary Saint Joseph of the Mountain, where he met and befriended Rutilio Grande, SJ Rutilio would serve as master of ceremonies when Romero was ordained bishop April 21, 1970.⁵¹

After being named bishop, Romero was named secretary of the Episcopal Conference of Central America and Panama. During this time, Romero found himself caught in the middle of the debate concerning the application of Vatican II and the episcopal conference at Medellín. The archbishop Luis Chávez and his auxiliary bishop Arturo Rivera y Damas promoted the Council and Medellín, and attacked the inequality between rich and poor, as well as the issue of land ownership. Martin Maier notes that in 1971 "Romero made a 180 degree turn and distanced himself from the priests socially and politically committed."⁵² In May of 1975, Romero was named consultor for the Latin American Pontifical Commission. Here he spoke critically of the activities of the Jesuits in the University, especially the political theology of Ellacuría and what he termed the new Christology of Sobrino. He was also named bishop of Santiago de María. At the time, Romero took this opportunity to cement a more conservative line. But Maier argues that between 1975 and 1977 he began to be transformed by his experience with the people as bishop. He cites two Passionist priests who claim that direct contact with the poor, the repression he experienced with a massacre in his diocese, and contact with a center created after Medellín began to transform some of his more conservative leanings.⁵³

Before naming a new Archbishop to replace Chávez, the nuncio consulted forty people in the government, private enterprise and women of the higher classes. The consensus choice was Romero who was the hope of many wealthy people who thought he would guide the church back to a more spiritual place. The nuncio did not consult Archbishop Chávez, who certainly would have recommended his auxiliary bishop, Rivera. During this time, Jon Sobrino, as well as many others, feared that Romero would be conservative, strongly influenced by Opus Dei, against a more progressive stance in line with Medellín.⁵⁴ For this reason, Archbishop Romero received a rather cold reception when he was ordained on February 22, 1977. But the new Archbishop soon began winning people over. He appeared at the seminary and asked for everyone's help, even Father Ricardo Urioste who had not attended his ordination, yet was made the new Vicar General.

The death of Rutilio Grande on March 12, 1977, greatly impacted the new Archbishop. John Dear writes that Romero's conversion really occurred with the death of Rutilio Grande.⁵⁵ Sobrino, present at the funeral mass which Romero insisted on celebrating in the middle of the night, claims that the death of Rutilio opened the eyes of the new Archbishop. Salvador Carranza compares the significance of Rutilio to Romero, to that which John the Baptist had on Jesus. The killing of the first native Salvadoran priest caused Romero to mandate that one Mass be celebrated in the entire Archdiocese on the twentieth of March as a sign of protest. Over 100,000 people attended the Mass, which spilled out from the cathedral into the main square and surrounding streets. In this Mass, Romero preached that it is Christ who evangelizes and gives his body and blood for the world in the Eucharist and "The only force that can save is Jesus who speaks to us of the real liberation."[56]

But Romero also tried to be a force of reconciliation. When a government minister was kidnaped, Mauricio Borgonovo Pohl, the Archbishop tried to help in the negotiations. When the minister's body was found, Romero presided at the funeral, as well as at the funeral of Father Alfonso Navarro the following day.[57] Maier claims that within the first three months, Archbishop Romero had transformed into a different bishop, one who looked to encounter the people and to suffer as they suffered. Romero turned down the offer of some businessmen who wanted to build a new palace for the Archbishop. Instead Romero moved out of the traditional residence and into a small room in the cancer section of a hospital for the indigent poor. The sisters who lived there would construct a special set of rooms for him on the 1st floor, which he moved into on August 15, his birthday. In December of 1978, Romero was nominated for the Nobel prize by 118 members of the British parliament, but Mother Theresa of Calcutta would win the prize in 1979. In 1978 and 1979, Monseñor fought many battles, but mostly with the conservative government, bishops in El Salvador who didn't support him, and even with Rome. Sobrino writes about Romero during this time period, and was impressed by the way he confronted the repression. After a young Jesuit was captured Romero refused to sign a letter saying he was not mistreated. After the army entered Aguilares expelling three Jesuits and killing hundreds of *campesinos*, he went there to denounce the atrocities. In his homily in Aguilares Romero prophetically preached, "You have converted the town into a jail and a place of torture."[58]

Romero made a big impact on the theologians, and the Jesuits who worked at the UCA at that time. Ignacio Ellacuría, Rodolfo Cardenal, Jon Sobrino, and others would all speak and write articles supporting the stance of the Archbishop. Sobrino, for example, reflects back on the Eucharistic Procession in Aguilares, when people paused in front of the soldier's guarding the mayor's office and the Archbishop yelled out "Go Ahead," prompting them to walk straight past the soldier and the mayor's office. Sobrino remarks, "I also remember that day the impact Monseñor Romero had for my own theology. The way he celebrated the Eucharist was for me a revelation; and was . . . a kind of (Eucharistic) theology class. All of the theological themes were known, but Mons. Romero elaborated them *in actu* with such truth and creativity that he explained what the Eucharist is better than many long years of study."[59] Scholars continue to study Romero's homilies and writings. As his canonization process continues it will be interesting to see if he might also be named a Doctor of the Church in addition to being named a martyr.[60] Gustavo Gutiérrez says the main task of the theology of liberation is to tell the poor that God loves them. Regardless of whether or not he attains the status of respected theologian or Doctor of the Church, Romero had a great love for the poor, and attempted through his teaching office as bishop to explain how much God loves them.

Sobrino writes fondly about the last time he saw the Archbishop, when Sobrino returned from a meeting of bishops and theologians in Sao Paulo, Brazil, in February of 1980.[61] Pedro Casaldaliga sent words of encouragement with Sobrino with his return to El Salvador and Romero responded with a letter on March 24 just a few hours before his death. In the letter, he thanks the Brazilian bishop for his backing and hopes their fraternal mission continues "to be an expression of the hopes and anguish of the poor, happy to run with Jesus the same risks, for identifying ourselves with the causes of the dispossessed. In the light of the faith, I feel completely united in affect, prayer, and the triumph of the Resurrection."[62] In the last month of his life, Romero consciously chose to run the same risks as the poor. By standing in solidarity with the poor, Romero would make the ultimate sacrifice.

Starting in February of 1980, Romero received almost continuous death threats. In spite of these death threats he continued to denounce the repression in his preaching. In the Sunday homily on February 24 Romero proclaimed,

> I take advantage of this first Sunday of Lent . . . to energetically protest for this new repressive act, which is not only against the Church, but also goes directly against the people, already what the authors of this attempt want to avoid is that the people will know the truth, that they have criteria to judge what is happening in the country, and reach a unity to say definitively, "Enough!," and to put an end to the exploitation and domination of the Salvadoran oligarchy.[63]

Near the end of the homily he challenges the rich and claims that with real liberation comes human dignity and human rights. Romero preaches, "When (the powerful) try to torture, kill, massacre so that the powerful might subjugate, what tremendous idolatry they are offering to the god of power, the god of money. So many victims, so much blood, that God, the real God, the author of life of the people, will collect from them a great sum for the idolatry of power."[64] This homily and others representative of these last few months made some people, especially those rich in wealth or with ties to right wing political power, very uncomfortable. Delgado reports that the very rich and powerful in the country, many in the military, and even some bishops who accused Romero of being a subversive, were all in agreement—Romero had to go.[65]

Forty-eight hours before his death, a team of Romero's closest counselors met to discuss his Sunday homily and a letter he had received signed by forty priests asking if he would soften the tone of his denouncements, and instead concentrate on a message of hope. Delgado was with a group of people who lunched with Romero the day before the homily, and at one point tears formed in Romero's eyes, as he spoke about his closest friends, both priests and laity, and shared with them about the seriousness of the death threats.[66] Many had never seen him so sad, and one woman suggested he take more precautions for his own safety. Near the end of his last Sunday homily, Romero made a special plea to the military. Monseñor spoke gravely,

> I would like to make a call in a special manner to the men of the Army, and concretely to the bases of the National Guard, to the police, and to the jails: Brothers, you are of our same people, you kill your own campesino brothers and, against the order to kill another man, should prevail the law of God which says: "Do not kill." No soldier is obligated to obey an order against the law of God. An immoral law, no one should complete it. Already it is time to recover your conscience . . . In the name of God, then, and in the name of this suffering people, whose wailing rises to the heavens each day more tumultuous, I beg you, I pray to you, I order you in the name of God: Stop the repression![67]

The next morning, Romero went to pray and celebrate mass for the sisters in the hospital as was his usual custom. Delgado reports that he vested for mass in a lightweight white alb, which normally was the signal that he was going to the beach. The sisters joked with the Archbishop that he should take them with him. He purportedly responded, "Where I am going, you cannot go."[68] That morning the death threats increased, and even the Jesuit radio station at the UCA received threats for airing the homily, one official saying that the Archbishop's words were in fact a crime. The sisters were right, and the Archbishop did in fact spend the day at the beach with some priest friends. On the way back he stopped by Santa Tecla, and went to confession with his spiritual director who lived there.[69] They dropped him off at the sisters's place at the hospital of the Divine Providence, and he just had enough time to shower before mass. The mass began promptly at six, and after the homily a shot rang out which would take his life.[70] He fell to the ground and several sisters rushed to his side attempting to revive him. He was rushed to the clinic, but it was too late. During mass the next day, Father Ricardo Urioste expressed what most people were feeling, "They have killed our father, they have killed our pastor, they have killed our prophet and killed our guide. It is as if each one of us has lost a part of our own self."[71]

Sobrino speaks of the death of Romero as if it were the death of a mentor or spiritual father. At the very least the life and death of Monseñor Romero greatly influences Sobrino's theology. Sobrino sees Romero as following in the line of Medellín and Puebla, especially concerning liberation from all types of slavery and the preferential option for the poor. In Oscar Romero, we find an example of the word of God who wants to unify the church and its people, in a sense the "word of God" for El Salvador.[72] In addition, Monseñor Romero's actions and words continue to inspire theologians to find meaning in his death. Sobrino suggests that theologians should be inspired to find "the presence of God in the poor, and the faith of the poor and the martyrs."[73] Situating Christian theology in the place of the poor proves to be a novel methodological approach. I think Romero gives theologians a starting point for their reflection. Christian theology should be done with and for the poor. Romero also shows the importance a life of conversion. Theologians should consider that they are providing a service to others, a service which requires humility, gratitude, and the enjoyment of truth and evangelization. Romero always hoped his time as Archbishop would affirm that God loves us and wants to save us. With his life and death, Romero provides theologians a starting point, a location and a trajectory.

THE U.S. CHURCHWOMEN IN EL SALVADOR

With the election of Ronald Reagan in the 1980 November elections, the violence again escalated sharply in El Salvador. The army looked forward to the promise of more military aid, and a more favorable President than under the Carter regime, known for its positive human rights record. Hundreds of *campesinos* were killed by the death squads, who even targeted lay church leaders such as catechists, parish council members, and leaders in Christian base ecclesial communities.[74] (CEBs) Since the mid-1970s foreign missionaries from Spain, France, the United States and other countries had been harassed and were at risk for deportation. Parishioners and even children in their youth groups were sometimes stopped by army patrols or right-wing paramilitary groups and interrogated as to whether priests and religious were training members of the guerrilla or harboring weapons.[75] This situation increased after 1980.

Four U.S. churchwomen were missioned to El Salvador and attempted to work and minister in the midst of this civil war. Whole books have been written about the lives of Ita Ford, Jean Donovan, Dorothy Kazel, and Maura Clarke. I will focus more narrowly on the events leading up to their deaths, the significance of their deaths in El Salvador, and their relation to Romero and the Jesuits in El Salvador.[76] Ita Ford and Maura Clarke, Maryknoll Sisters, were missioned to work in Chalatenango in the remote northern region of El Salvador, one of the hardest hit regions before and during the civil war. In 1980 the region also suffered greatly from the effects of a hurricane. Dorothy Kazel, an Ursuline sister, and Jean Donovan, a Maryknoll Missioner, worked in the areas surrounding the port city of La Libertad, a parish which even today has one main church in town with over fifty countryside chapels and 50,000 parishioners, with only four priests to attend them.[77] All of these women knew each other since they attended national and diocesan meetings of religious and lay missionaries. In fact they had a small reunion in La Libertad, when Maura arrived in the country after having served in Nicaragua for many years.[78] In November, after the drowning death of Sister Carla, a Maryknoll sister who worked with Ita Ford in Chalatenango, Dorothy, Jean, Maura and Ita all gathered at a little beach house near La Libertad, to grieve, recoup, and plan their next mission strategies. While they were all aware of the escalating violence, they did not believe that they themselves were in immediate danger. The thought was since Jean and Maura were blonde haired and blue eyed, they would not have any trouble with roadblocks.[79] In the meantime, the Assumption sisters working in Chalatenango began receiving death threats, and moved out of their convent and into the residence of Maura and Ita. In late November, Ita and Maura made plans to attend a regional conference for members of their order. Dorothy and Jean agreed to pick them up at the airport on December 2.

Meanwhile back in Chalatenango on December first, the sacristan of the parish where the sisters served was discreetly called aside by a friend and shown a death list which had his name, the names of the parish driver, cook, Father Efraim Lopez, the Assumption Sisters, Maura and Ita. That same day, Father Lopez received a letter accusing all the Church workers of being communists, stirring up trouble, and turning the people against the government.[80] After a meeting of twenty-two Maryknoll sisters from Panama, Nicaragua and El Salvador, Maura and Ita, unaware of the threats, started their trek back to El Salvador. Four Maryknoll sisters, Teresa Alexander, Madeline Dorsey, Maura Clarke and Ita Ford were inconveniently booked on separate flights. Unfortunately this poor scheduling would mean an extra round trip to the airport for Sister Dorothy Kazel and Jean Donovan.[81] At 4:00 on December second, Dorothy and Jean picked up Madeline and Teresa and took them back to their jeep, which they had left in La Libertad. Unbeknownst to them, a National Guardsman on duty was watching the women, and placed a call to his local commander. When Jean and Maura returned to meet the 6:00 flight, they found it was delayed an hour. The local guardsman made another call, and the local commander dispatched five guardsmen for an unspecified mission.[82]

Finally, at about 7:00, the flight from Managua arrived, and as soon as Ita and Maura cleared customs, the four churchwomen piled into the church van and drove off for La Libertad. They were never seen alive again. Most likely they were taken to a nearby guard station, where they were raped and tortured. From the guard station, they were driven up a remote road past the village of San Pedro Nauhalco.[83] About six kilometers up this remote dirt road, they were ordered out of the vehicle, shot and killed, and left alongside the road. The next morning local police were called, and they came and buried the bodies.[84] In the early morning hours of December 4, thirty-six hours after the women had disappeared, the parish at La Libertad received the horrible news. Since parish and Maryknoll officials had been planning to meet with Ambassador White that day, they called him to see if he would meet them at the burial site. Two of the embassy security men went down to the local justice of the peace to get permission to dig up the bodies.[85] The first body they found was Jean Donovan, then Maura, then Dorothy and finally Ita. Ambassador White was fuming with rage and remarked, "We're going to do this one right. We're not going to let the military get away with this."[86] In fact, Salvadoran government officials never really cooperated, and once Carter left office, the case was never fully investigated by the government, military or National Guard, who were of course complicit in their deaths. In the tradition of the Maryknoll Missioners, Maura and Ita are buried in Chalatenango, the place where they ministered. Dorothy Kazel is buried in Cleveland near her Mother House, and Jean Donovan was buried in Sarasota, FL where her parents had retired.[87]

The deaths of these four religious women had an immediate effect on the international awareness of the problems in El Salvador and especially in the United States. While the official State Department position, submitted as testimony to the Senate Committee by Alexander Haig, claimed that the sisters had run a road block, we now know that Ita Ford and Maura Clarke were most likely the targets, and that they probably never even got in the van. While U.S. military aid was slowed because of the attention for a time, as early as January 1981 the portion of military aid that had been suspended in December was resumed. While the deaths of these committed missionaries did bring international attention for a time, the attention did not greatly impact the death squads and government forces who continued to carry out a mission of intimidation, torture and massacre. These four women are still remembered and revered in the communities where they ministered, and by various groups in the United States. But outside of Chalatenango, La Libertad, the small community near San Pedro, and intellectual communities like the UCA, in the city of San Salvador and in many regions of the country, these four women have been like many anonymous martyrs, largely forgotten.

Jon Sobrino includes them in his litany of martyrs, as exemplary women who died for their faith. He claims that they form part "of an interminable list of priests, seminarians, students, campesinos, workers, professionals and intellectuals."[88] Sobrino writes with indignation as he paraphrases the psalm "How Long, Oh Lord" and at the same time a decisive resolve in the promise of what is to come: "Be Joyful Jerusalem, liberation is at hand."[89] Sobrino both laments the loss of these four missionary women, and hopes for the coming liberation of all Salvadorans. These four courageous women provide yet another example of just and innocent women who are assassinated and thus exemplify Christ crucified. Sobrino enumerates, "This time Christ who has died (can be seen) in these four women, religious, and North American. And for this (reason) the darkness of this crime is accompanied by a special light . . . These four *women* are Christ who died."[90] The bodies of these four women represent all the men and women who have been deprived of their human rights and oppressed in El Salvador. They illuminate the path to liberation. In a special way, these four sisters "have united the Salvadoran people by uniting with the Salvadoran woman. A woman who is the creator of fortitude does not abandon the one who suffers, just as these four sisters did not abandon the people, in spite of serious threats."[91]

These four religious women embody Jesus Christ, and give the people of El Salvador an example of the good the United States can bring to El Salvador. Instead of the almighty dollar, imperial goals, and exploitation, they brought faith in Jesus, love of neighbor, and a search for justice. These religious sisters reminded the highest dignitaries sent by President Carter to El Salvador, that not only an investigation into the deaths of these four women is needed, but also an investigation into the genocide of 10,000 Salvadorans! Theologians and like-minded Salvadorans welcome all Christians who are like the sisters, and, for the attitude that led to their martyrdom, the Church in El Salvador can "only thank them from the deepest part of its heart."[92] It is possible to see not just Christ crucified, but also the Risen Christ in these four women. They give the Salvadoran people hope in their eventual liberation. They are a visible sign of the presence of God and so the last word should be a prayer of thanksgiving. Sobrino writes, "Our last word must be thanks. With Maura, Ita, Dorothy and Jean, God passed through El Salvador."[93] Indeed, this is high praise, since the same phrase God passed through El Salvador is often associated with Oscar Romero. These four women represent both Christ crucified and Christ resurrected and for this reason are examples of Jesuanic martyrs, a term that will be defined in greater detail in later chapters.

MARTYRS OF THE UCA

In November there were rumors in the capital of an imminent Farabundo Martí National Liberation Front (FMLN) offensive. For this reason the military was on high alert and installed government checkpoints to all major entrances to the city. There were also patrols in the neighborhoods surrounding the Jesuit University. On November 13, Salvadoran military forces entered the UCA, the Jesuit University José Simeon Cañas under the pretext of looking weapons. They entered the Jesuit community and conducted a room by room search. The soldiers left, having done minimal damage to the Jesuit residence. It was later suspected that this was in fact a reconnaissance mission, and they were looking for Ignacio Ellacuría, the university rector's room. Ellacuría was not home at the time of the search. In the following days, the number of troops increased in the area, and especially around the UCA.[94]

Joe Mulligan, S.J. describes that on November 15, "an army officer posted in the UCA neighborhood commented to a Jesuit that there was going to be a lot of movement in the afternoon or evening. About 3:00 p.m. some 120–130 members of the Atlacatl (battalion) entered Loyola Center, the Jesuit retreat house . . . At about 7:00 p.m., after the fall of curfew, the men moved out and headed down to the UCA campus."[95] At 11:00 p.m. on November 15, a small group stayed after a meeting of the Joint Command at their headquarters. The Defense Minister's report states that all of the members of the high command were present, including President Cristiani. At the same time, Lt. Espinoza was ordered to report to Col. Benavides in the Military Academy where he was told, "This is a situation where it is us or them; we are going to begin with the ringleaders. Within our sector we have the university and Ellacuría is there."[96] Over fifty soldiers would enter the UCA campus that night, though not all played a direct part in the assassination. Some of the soldiers entered the Theological Reflection Center, now the Centro Monseñor Romero, and burned parts of the offices, machine gunned computers, shot up a portrait of Romero, and burned another in effigy. Between 1:00 and 2:00 A.M. they pounded at the outside door of the Jesuit residence. Segundo Montes, the superior of the community, cried out to them that they could enter at the main door and he would open it for them.[97] Five of the Jesuit community members were led out to the lawn outside the community, while López y López the head of *Fe y Alegría* remained asleep. The soldiers began to search the rest of the house, and found Elba and Celina Ramos the daughter and wife of the caretaker, who had asked if they could sleep in the Jesuit community. The caretaker's house had taken some shrapnel from a bombing near the UCA wall just a few days earlier and they were afraid to stay the night there when they saw an increase in the number of soldiers in the neighborhood around the campus. Elba Ramos was the cook at the Jesuit theologate, a residence for Jesuits completing the theology requirements for priesthood, which is about a kilometer uphill from the UCA campus. She and her daughter had decided to spend the night rather than cross all of the roadblocks and avoid any violence since there had been rumors of a guerilla attack.

The five Jesuits were ordered to lie down on the grass outside the community. Martín-Baró cried out in a loud voice, "This is an abomination, and you are all scum."[98] When the order was given, all five Jesuits were fatally shot in the back of the head and some were also shot multiple times in the torso. Elba and Celina were also shot by soldiers outside their rooms simultaneously.[99] The Jesuits were all fatally wounded by the head shots; the other bullets only added to the effect. Upon hearing the shots, Father López y López, the only native Salvadoran priest home at the time, woke up and walked out the door to see what was happening. He cried out to the soldiers and pleaded for his life saying he was not important and they did not need to kill him. He was shot once in the heart, and as the soldier approached, he grabbed his ankle. Apparently in fear, the soldier then emptied his gun into the priest's chest.[100] The soldiers dragged Father Moreno, SJ back into the house, but into the wrong room, the room of Jon Sobrino. When his body was found, a copy of the book *The Crucified God* by Jurgen Moltmann had fallen from Sobrino's desk, and was soaked in Moreno's blood.[101] At the end of the shooting, the soldiers shot off a Bengal light, which was the signal to withdraw. Some of the soldiers in the Theological Center hastily wrote FMLN on some of the walls, attempting to blame the rebel forces for the deaths.

The horrific tale of the murder of these six Jesuits and these two women, Ignacio Ellacuría, Segundo Montes, Ignacio Martín-Baró, Amando Lopez, Juan Ramón Moreno, Joaquín López y López, Elba, and Celina Ramos, quickly spread throughout Latin America and the rest of the world. Both Pope John Paul II and Fr. General Peter Hans Kolvenbach, SJ immediately sent letters expressing their shock and dismay at the murders.[102] Father José María Tojeira, SJ preached at the funeral mass on November 19:

> Because they sought the truth and proclaimed that part of the truth they were finding, they were assassinated, like so many others in El Salvador, like Archbishop Romero. They were killed because that truth helped the poor . . . Their testimony to the truth has now been sealed with blood in their death. This is the last word which our brothers have spoken, as a community, as martyrs . . . Their death, in the midst of the blood of the people, has joined them to that suffering face of the Lord Jesus which is seen today in Latin America in the faces of the marginalized of our cities, the peasant without land . . . the persecuted and those killed because they worked so that the gospel would become life in our people.[103]

Just like some of the earlier murders in El Salvador, great lengths were taken to cover up the perpetrators of the crimes. Initial reports claimed that the FMLN was responsible for the deaths, since Ellacuría had recently criticized them. But this later backfired, when Major Eric Buckland, the senior U.S. military advisor attached to C-5 (Psych-Ops) caused Cristiani to release a statement in January announcing that the Salvadoran Armed Forces were responsible for the murders.[104]

The day of the murders three members of the Jesuit community were not present. Rodolfo Cardenal, SJ had decided to stay in Santa Tecla with the Jesuit community there when he saw the number of soldiers and government troops surrounding the UCA. Jon Cortina, SJ had tried to return from Chalatenango, but local community leaders would not let him leave the city because they feared for his safety.[105] The third member not present was Jon Sobrino, SJ who was in Thailand when he heard about the deaths. Sobrino said he was first awakened by an Irish priest and when asked to sit down to take the call from London, he expected to hear that Ellacuría had been killed. But when he heard each name he began writing them down one by one, and could not believe that almost his entire community had been murdered. The last two names of the women simply outraged him.[106] One cannot imagine how Sobrino must have felt: had he been home, he would have been one of the victims. Sobrino himself found it difficult to cope during those days. He writes, "I spent several hours, or rather several days, unable to react . . . The distance made me feel helpless and alone. And the six murdered Jesuits were my community, they were really my family. We had lived, worked, suffered, and enjoyed ourselves together for many years. Now they were dead."[107] He would later question why he was alive and why he was worthy to live on, but that was also transformed into a sense of mission and purpose: to finish the book he and Ignacio Ellacuría were writing together, to finish Juan Ramón Moreno's next issue of *Revista Latinoamericano de Teología*, and to return to the UCA and El Salvador. The reactions from around the world gave Sobrino great comfort, from Archbishop Rivera, to the Superior General who promised to come to the UCA for Christmas. With this tremendous support, Sobrino also gained the courage to return, not just for his Jesuit brothers, Elba and Celina, but also for the 70,000 other victims in El Salvador.[108]

In his short book *Companions of Jesus: The Jesuit Martyrs of El Salvador*, Sobrino describes the lives of each of his companions and ends the descriptive chapter by naming them as martyrs. The papal nuncio at their funeral mass called them martyrs, and Sobrino calls them Jesuanic martyrs, just as he calls Rutilio Grande, SJ, Archbishop Romero, the Churchwomen from the United States Jesuanic martyrs.[109] As chapters 5 and 6 will elucidate, Sobrino's writing on martyrdom shows a marked shift after these events. While he continues to write about a number of important themes from Medellín and Puebla, he develops these themes with more fervor and gusto after the impact of the death of his community and their two collaborators after 1989. The deaths of these significant people and the impact on his theological work cannot be underestimated.

EL MOZOTE

While the case studies of the martyrs point toward an expansion of the definition of martyrdom, the larger situation of violence in El Salvador (and other places in Latin America) suggests that we also consider expanding the category of those who have suffered martyrdom to include not just those individually targeted but also the targets of mass violence. Including the El Mozote massacre which occurred during the Salvadoran civil war may seem controversial. But as chapter 6 will demonstrate, this story of violence and other similar stories from the Salvadoran civil war represent the possibility of anonymous martyrs, and El Mozote is an emblematic case. In December of 1981, the FMLN warned people of the area of Mozote in Morazán that a military invasion was imminent. Because the people were largely evangelical Christians and were not FMLN sympathizers they felt they had nothing to fear from the army. But on December 11, "the U.S. trained Atlacatl Brigade rounded up the people, separated the men, women and children, and executed them. The number of people killed in Mozote and the surrounding villages number over 700."[110] This massacre, and others which did not lessen in frequency until the change of government in 1984, terrorized the civilian population. Most of those killed in the massacres were not active guerrilla fighters but civilians. It is possible to recount many more horror stories of massacres in different parts of the country such as the River Sumpul, the massacres in bombings in Chalatenango and in the countryside near Apopa. With the election of a more centrist President in Duarte in 1984, some of the human rights violations stopped and there were fewer recorded massacres. The Catholic Church also softened its criticism of the new government. But the fact remains that there were many innocent Christians and other noncombatants slaughtered during this brutal civil war. Some can be accounted for, while many others remain nameless.

CONCLUSION

In sum, the reality of martyrdom in Latin America in general and in El Salvador in particular provide powerful material for reflection on the significance of martyrdom and what constitutes a martyr in the late twentieth and now twenty-first century. There is a broader Latin American reality beyond the scope of El Salvador. From the tip of South America in Chile to the northern most part of Mexico, the past century illustrates how the political situation in various countries affected the church. There are many Latin American countries which now claim their share of martyrs from the past century. This may appear at the outset to be an oddity, since almost all countries in Latin America are predominantly Catholic and Christian. Nevertheless, many men and women have died and some due to the way they lived out the values of their faith. The reality of El Salvador proves to be a glaring example of this problematic. These four exemplary cases—Rutilio Grande, Oscar Romero, the U.S. churchwomen, and the UCA Jesuits and their companions—depict the reality of martyrdom in El Salvador. While perhaps they may not comply in the strictest sense with the traditional definition of martyr in *odium fidei*, they do provide examples of men and women who died for their beliefs and their faith. These four examples were chosen because of their significance and in varying degrees most closely impact Sobrino and his theological writings. It is also important to account for those people who die for their faith, lay catechists, church workers and others, who never get mentioned so prominently. These more anonymous martyrs impact the discussion of the war in El Salvador and provide fuel for the discussion of their theological significance for the church.

It is now necessary to explore the theological impact and the importance of expanding the meaning of martyrdom in the twenty-first century. The above case studies will be referred to often and it is possible to imagine many other more recent martyrs as well. For example, Archbishop Girardi in Guatemala, Sister Dorothy Stang in Brazil, and others who have died while living out the values of their Christian faith. Martyrdom is and continues to be a reality in Latin America today.

NOTES

1. See Rutilio Grande: *Martir De La Evangelizacion Rural En El Salvador*. San Salvador, El Salvador: UCA Editores, 1978, for a brief synopsis of his life before the Jesuits and with the Society of Jesus.
2. For a more in depth study of Rutilio Grande's life see Cardenal, Rodolfo. *Historia De Una Esperanza: Vida De Rutilio Grande*. San Salvador, El Salvador: UCA Editores, 1985. Cardenal probes into the psychological make-up of Rutilio Grande but the book remains untranslated.
3. While much of this information is in several biographies, only Carranza notes this fact.
4. Thomas M. Kelly emphasizes this pastoral plan in his book *When The Gospel Grows Feet: An Ecclesiology in Context*.
5. *When The Gospel Grows Feet*, 110.
6. *Rutilio Grande: Martir De La Evangelizacion Rural En El Salvador*, 26. There is a great chart on this page which outlines the major events in his life from birth until death.
7. Tilo was the common nickname for someone named Rutilio.

8. *Rutilio Grande: Martir De La Evangelizacion Rural En El Salvador*, 40. Rutilio termed it *un crísis teológico* which he tried to resolve through some debate with the bishops. His Jesuit superiors were more receptive to the "new theology" erupting from the Council.

9. Ibid, 43. Rutilio wrote during this period of "el escandalo cuando un poco tienen el goce de los bienes" in several letters. The term "marxismo recalentado" was not reserved solely for R. Grande, SJ but for anyone who spoke out against social injustices or social structures controlled by the oligarchy.

10. Ibid, 46. Cardenal notes that this was a painful process for Rutilio, especially since many of these bishops he had previously considered friends, or at least worked with and enjoyed a fraternal spirit. The expulsion from the seminary of three seminarians who had worked with Padre Grande pastorally on weekends didn't help either. See Cardenal's *Historia de la Esperanza*, 134. Cardenal uses the nickname Tilo predominantly in his book.

11. Ibid, 48. The Institute in Quito was called *El Instituto de Pastoral Latinoamericano*.

12. Ibid, 49. Translated from the original Spanish "un trabajo pastoral en equipo, en una zona rural campesina o sub-urbana marginada en órden a una promoción integral a partir de una concientización cristiana." I insert "of values" because an integral promotion literally translated has little meaning in English. Letter to Vice-Provincial June 27, 1972, and the idea copied in a letter to an Ecuadoran Jesuit July 23, 1973.

13. *When the Gospel Grows Feet*, 147. For those interested in the implementation of this pastoral plan see especially chapters 7 and 8 in this book.

14. Ibid, 148.

15. *Rutilio Grande: Martir De La Evangelizacion Rural En El Salvador*, 55. "Curas comunistas" or communist priests was part of the rhetoric of right wing groups. Rutilio's initial response to the charge: "Jesús también era subversivo" or "Jesus was also subversive."

16. Ibid, 54. In Spanish, "Jesús está con nosotros cuando denunciamos las injusticias." Throughout this book I will simply use the Spanish word *campesinos*, because the dictionary translation "simple peasants" has a derogatory sense in English, and "those from the countryside" does not fully sum up their social reality.

17. Ibid, 59.

18. Ibid, 61. For his pastoral ministry in Aguilares there is a twentieth anniversary commemoration book designed for *campesinos*, with pictures and a simple storyline. See Carranza, Salvador. *Una Luz Grande Nos Brillo: Rutilio Grande, SJ* San Salvador, El Salvador: UCA Editores, 1997. The book was made possible by a donation from the Boston College Jesuit Community and is dedicated to BC President Donald Monan, SJ 1972–1996.

19. Ibid, 61. The census results between 1961 and 1973 indicate that the average person's calorie intake decreased from 1,797 to 1683. The minimum daily calorie intake should be 2,200 for the average person.

20. Ibid, 64.

21. See Grande, Rutilio "Violencia Y Situación Social." ECA 262 (1970): 369–75. This short article led to some tough conversations with some of the more conservative seminary faculty and seminarians.

22. *Rutilio Grande: Martir*, 66. "Rutilio y su equipo entraron en esta área explosiva y conflictiva justamente en el momento en la sociedad salvadoreña las contradicciones se estaban volviendo más agudas."

23. *When the Gospel Grows Feet*, 150.

24. *Rutilio Grande: Martir*, 71. The excerpt from his homily on Mary as Servant in Spanish "la que ha sido elegida por los siglos como Reina, como la mujer bella y tipa, porque no le irán a tomar medidas, de cintura de avispa, ni ha comprado votos, de esos que mercan por ahí, en las fiestas y allá en el hotel Sheraton."

25. Ibid, 79. The phrase "una buena crisis galilea" appears multiple times in the homilies of Grande. While the idea is not Sobrino's own, it does show that Grande had contact with the UCA university Jesuit community, and that both he and the theologians there were mutually enriched. Sobrino himself still states publicly that he was personally inspired by "Tilo." The "crisis in Galilee" also appears in chapter 3 "Jesus in the Service of God's Kingdom" of *Christology at the Crossroads*.

26. Ibid, 84. The most prominent of these was FECCAS, Federation of Salvadoran Christian Campesinos, a non-partisan Christian group which tried to helped workers organize into collectives and helped them advocate for better pay and better working conditions.

27. Ibid, 85–87. Rutilio had direct access to both the Archbishop and to President Arturo Molina at the time. Rutilio may even have made an arrangement with Molina to keep him informed about things to avoid a possible repression against the people in the parish.

28. Ibid, 87. A right wing group Falange, stated that its objective was to rid the country of communist priests. This group was suspected in the beating, but no one was ever charged with the crime. Father Rafael ministered in the parish immediately bordering Aguilares.

29. Ibid, 91. Even the United Nations acknowledged the fraud claims.

30. Ibid, 93.

31. Ibid, 104. Material in this paragraph relies heavily on Carranza's interpretation of events, since he was one of the Jesuit scholastics working with Grande, SJ, at the time. Cardenal notes that John Murphy, a Benedictine priest from the U.S. was also forced to leave the country at this time, due to pressure from the nuncio, and in order to avoid arrest and torture before deportation. *Historia de una Esperanza*, 555.

32. Ibid, 107. In this homily, Tilo uses the phrase "los Caines" referring to the Genesis account of Cain and Abel. He preached against those who would act against their brother with violence both overt and covert. This phrase was picked up and used by other Jesuit priests and religious in the years to come, "the Cains" of El Salvador who kill their brothers and sisters. Mario Bernal was the parish priest who served in Apopa and was deported.

33. Ibid, 109. Accounts differ as to the identities of these children. Dean Brackley, SJ claimed that the identity of at least one of these children is known, but since the killers may still be at large, no one has come forward to testify and two of the kids, now adults, live in the United States. Interview November 25, 2009.

34. Ibid, 110. Cardenal notes that the vehicle was a Safari (jeep/truck), and that Don Manuel sat in the front middle, because they picked up Nelson Lemus, who sat next in the right front seat next to the window, *Historia de una Esperanza*, 572.

35. Ibid. Cardenal's account differs slightly, and claims that Benito Estrada was clearly involved. When Benito got to the vehicle the children were screaming, and he let them out. They all ran away and one of them claims to have heard one more gunshot. Cardenal also notes that Manuel's body was inclined over Rutilio as if to protect him. *Historia De Una Esperanza*, 574.

36. Ibid, 111. Dean Brackley, SJ asserts that the children who currently live in the United States fled the country due to their fear for personal safety. Since the perpetrators of the crime have still not been charged, nor convicted, the details of this conversation cannot be put in writing. Interview with Dean Brackley, November 26, 2009.

37. Ibid, 117.

38. Romero Homily, March 14, 1977, Funeral Mass of Rutilio Grande, Cavada, Miguel, ed. *Homilías: Monsenor Oscar A. Romero*. Vol. 1. San Salvador, El Salvador: UCA Editores, 2005, 32. "Qué aporta la Iglesia a esta lucha universal por la liberación de tanta miseria?"

39. *Homilías: Romero*, 35. "Queremos decirles, hermanos criminales, que cayeron ya en la excomunión, están eschuchando en un radio . . . queremos decirles, hermanos criminales, que los amamos y que le pedimos a Dios el arrepentimiento para sus corazones, porque la Iglesis no es capaz de odiar, no tiene enemigos. El amor del Señor inspira la acción de Rutilio Grande."

40. Ibid, 153. During the calendar year of 1977 Aguilares becomes a symbol, so the "road to Aguilares" becomes synonymous with a Salvadoran way of the cross. Spanish: "illuminando a tantos en los caminos hacia Aguilares."

41. It is perhaps important to note that there were priests killed previously in El Salvador, but they were all of differing nationalities, Spanish, Panamanian, etc. But Rutilio was in this way, a proto-martyr, at least of the conflict in the 1970s. For more on the link between Grande and Romero see: Carranza, Salvador. *Romero-Rutilio: Vidas Encontradas*. San Salvador, El Salvador: UCA Editores, 1992.

42. Interview with Jon Sobrino, November 27, 2009.

43. Maier, Martin. *Monseñor Romero: Maestro De Espiritualidad*. San Salvador, El Salvador: UCA Editores, 2005. This book was originally written in German under the title: Maier, Martin. *Oscar Romero: Meister Der Spiritualitat*. Freiburg, Germany: Herder, 2001. For background on this section I draw primarily on pages 21–25.

44. Maier, 26. Maier does not go into as great of detail with this nickname, but Jesús Delgado uses this as a subheading in his first chapter and goes into great detail of his love of music. "El niño de la flauta." See Delgado, Jesus. *Oscar A. Romero: Biografía*. 2nd ed. San Salvador, El Salvador: UCA Editores, 1994, especially Chapter One.

45. Maier, 26–27.

46. Maier, 27. Martin Maier notes that Romero excelled in a panegyric competition in the seminary. These panegyrics were prepared expositions and common in Jesuit formation. Often the person was asked to prepare a discourse on particular saint or blessed of the Society of Jesus or the Catholic Church.

47. Ibid, 28. "ser con Cristo, un crucificado que redime. Con Cristo ser un resucitado que reparte resurección y vida." Maier does not cite where he found this short article written in 1940.

48. Maier, 30. "Le sacaba limosna a los ricos para dársela a los pobres. Así, a los pobres les aliviaba sus problemas y a los ricos su conciencia."

49. Maier, 31. The word in Spanish is *ascendido* literally to ascend, or raise one's stature or position. He was also given the title of a prelate, and from this time forward called "Monseñor Romero."

50. Maier, 32. "Obediente al servicio de la Iglesia, debo partir a San Salvador . . . desde donde seguiré amando y haciendo."

51. Ibid. Both Maier and Delgado report that Grande and Romero maintained a close friendship, and it was difficult for Romero when he had to tell Rutilio that he would not be the new rector of the seminary.

52. Maier, 36. "Romero realizó un giro de 180 grados y se distanció de los sacerdotes comprometidos social y políticamente." He also wrote a letter of support for the military occupation of the national university, and caused a sensation in 1973 when he wrote a letter reproaching the Jesuits in the Externado San José for teaching marxism. The accusation ended up being investigated and found false, and later as Archbishop he asked for forgiveness.

53. These Passionist priests would later write about Romero and his contact with the poor in Díez, Zacarias and Macho, Juan. *En Santiago de María Me Topé con la Miseria: Dos años de la Vida de Mons. Romero: 1975–1976*. Archdiocese of Santiago de María: 1994.

54. Maier, 43. Sobrino recalls a homily from 1976 when Romero publically criticized "radical" Christologies, so the naming of Romero as bishop was not well received by Sobrino or others trying to implement Medellín. See also Sobrino, Jon. *Monseñor Romero*. 3rd ed. San Salvador, El Salvador: UCA Editores 1995, 14.

55. Dear, John, "Oscar Romero and non-violent Struggle for Justice," Pax Christi, 8. Sobrino also affirms this assertion, saying that the personal relationship with Rutilio had a big impact on the Archbishop, and terms the conversion as "the miracle of Rutilio" "el milagro de Rutilio," Sobrino, Jon. *Monseñor Romero*. 3rd ed. San Salvador, El Salvador: UCA Editores 1995, 19–20. Not all would agree. In an Interview Mons. Urioste claims that Romero had a slow transformation over time. Interview with Mons. Urioste, November, 2009.

56. Cavada, Miguel, ed. *Homilias: Monsenor Oscar A. Romero*. Vol. 1. San Salvador, El Salvador: UCA Editores, 2005, 39. "la misa es Cristo que evangeliza; la misa es Cristo que da su cuerpo y su sangre para la vida del mundo." "La única fuerza que puede salvar es Jesús, que nos habla de la verdadera liberación." Romero's homily at "La Misa Unica" March 20, 1977.

57. Maier, 50. The government would assert that the church had something to do with the death of Borgonovo Pohl, and Navarro was apparently killed in retaliation. The killers of Navarro allegedly cried out "Be a patriot, kill a priest." "Haga patria. ¡Mate un cura!"

58. Maier, 34. "Conviertieron un pueblo en una cárcel y en un lugar de tortura."

59. Maier, 37. "Y también recuerdo de aquel día el impacto que me causó Mons. Romero para mi propia teología. La forma como celebró aquella eucaristía fue para mí muy reveladora; fue también . . . como una clase de teología. En aquella celebración fueron apareciendo los temas traditionales de la teología de la eucharistía . . .

pero Mons. Romero los elaboró in actu con tanta verdad y tanta creatividad que me esclarecieron qué es la eucharistía mejor que largos años de estudio."

60. Father Bob Pelton, CSC, recently mentioned that as he works with those in charge of the canonization process they are scouring his writings to support this case. Interview with Bob Pelton, CSC, May 31, 2016.

61. Sobrino, Jon. *Monseñor Romero*. 3rd ed. San Salvador, El Salvador: UCA Editores 1995, 46. Sobrino claims that the Archbishop was also invited to this gathering, but did not want to leave the country because of the intensifying violence.

62. Sobrino, *Monseñor Romero*, 47. "siendo expresión de las esperanzas y angustias de los pobres, alegres de correr como Jesús los mismos riesgos, por identificarnos con las causas de los disposeídos. A la luz de la fe, siéntame estrechamente unido en el afecto, la oración y el triunfo de la Resurrección."

63. Cavada, Miguel, ed. *Homilias: Monsenor Oscar A. Romero*. Vol. 6. San Salvador, El Salvador: UCA Editores, 2009, 302. Sunday February 24, 1980. The oligarchy which Romero refers to is the elite families of El Salvador who possessed most of the wealth of the country and thus influenced the government and military greatly.

64. Ibid, 309. "Cuando se trata de torturar, de matar, de masacrar para que se subyuguen los hombres al poder, qué tremenda idolatría que le está ofreciendo al dios poder, al dios dinero. Tantas víctimas, tanta sangre, que Dios, el verdadero Dios, el autor de la vida de los hombres, se lo va a cobrar bien caro a esos idólatras del poder." I add the phrase (the powerful) because it is inferred from the context of the previous sentence, *los poderosos*.

65. Delgado, Jesus. *Oscar A. Romero: Biografía*. 2nd ed. San Salvador, El Salvador: UCA Editores, 1994, 198.

66. Ibid, 186. Delgado insinuates that even some conservative bishops backed the plan to assassinate the Archbishop, though he cites no letters or testimony as evidence.

67. Cavada, *Homilias: Monsenor Oscar A. Romero*. Vol. 6. 453. A more complete theological analysis of the great theological treasure found in Romero's homilies, pastoral letters, and spiritual diary still needs to be completed. Perhaps as his cause for sainthood continues this work will be done. The focus on Romero tends to be on his martyrdom, and some in El Salvador for political and ecclesiological reasons still want to deny some of the theology behind his impressive homilies.

68. Delgado, *Oscar A. Romero: Biografía*, 202. While Delgado is the only one to report this banter between Romero and the sisters, I have no reason to doubt it. Maier does not quote it, but notes that many in El Salvador speak of the similarity between Jesus' last hours, knowing he would die, and Romero's last hours.

69. Maier, *Monseñor Romero: Maestro De Espiritualidad*, 84. Maier does not mention if this confession was an aberration, or a normal occurrence for his day off.

70. Delgado, *Oscar A. Romero: Biografía*, 205. Romero did not normally celebrate this mass, proof that the assassins had intimate knowledge and access to his comings and goings that day. This account is disputed. Gene Palumbo, a former *New York Times* correspondent in San Salvador, asserts that a newswoman who was there said the shot ran out immediately after the homily. This discounts the version the sisters at the Hospital give in their tour. Regardless of the version, Romero was killed after the homily and during the celebration of mass.

71. Maier, 86. Urioste was in charge of Romero's canonization process but died on January 16, 2016 in San Salvador at the age of 90 of natural causes.

72. Sobrino, *Monseñor Romero*, 173. "Mons. Romero fue *palabra de Dios* para El Salvador." Italics are Sobrino's emphasis. Obviously, Sobrino does not suggest that Romero was Jesus, the Word of God, but rather spoke prophetically to the people of El Salvador, and incarnated the word of God in an exemplary fashion.

73. Ibid, 178.

74. Often these lay church leaders were also preaching a message of social justice, peace and non-violence. They were targets because of their leadership. The death squads wanted to instill fear in the general population. The base communities are often known as "Comunidades de Base" or "Comunidades Eclesiales de Base" in Spanish. I will continue to abbreviate as CEBs.

75. Interview with Fr. Paul Schindler, Diocese of Cleveland, pastor of La Libertad parish 1972–1982, 2005 to present, December 2, 2009. Father Paul asserts that the soldiers knew the foreign missionaries had nothing to do with the guerrilla forces and never found any weapons at their parish or any of those run by Maryknoll missioners. The soldiers and right-wing paramilitary forces simply used it as an excuse for harassment. He was also incredibly helpful as a first hand source since he knows so many people, even U.S. embassy staff then and now.

76. For other resources on the four martyrs see: Zagano, Phyllis. *Ita Ford: Missionary Martyr*. New York: Paulist Press, 1996. Evans, Jeanne, ed. *Here I Am Lord: The Letters and Writings of Ita Ford*. New York: Orbis Books, 2005. Garcia, Maria Candelaria. *Un Legado De Amor*. 2nd ed. San Salvador: Impresas Quijanos, 2005. This list is by no means exhaustive.

77. Interview with Father Paul Schindler, December 2, 2009. The city of La Libertad and the surrounding region has long been associated with the "Cleveland Team" a mission team made up of priests from the Cleveland Diocese, religious sisters, and lay volunteer missioners.

78. Noone, Judith M. *The Same Fate as the Poor*. New York: Maryknoll Sisters Publication, 1984, 102, 115. Dorothy and Jean welcomed Maura to the country in La Libertad, and Ita came down from Chalatenango. After a series of meetings, Ita dropped Maura off at her new home in the Chalatenango region, and continued on to her remote community site, where she lived with Sister Carla. Carla would drown when their truck foundered in a rainy Chalatenango river in November of 1980. Ita Ford survived when Carla pushed her out of the car as it submerged.

79. *The Same Fate as the Poor*, 130. Some of the sisters said they were going to bleach their hair, after seeing how easy Jean and Maura passed through roadblocks. Father Paul Schindler noted that while Ita was very quiet, she was fearless in terms of advocating for people in her parish, and that Jean Donovan was equally fearless when it came to driving in the most desperate parts of the country.

80. Ibid, 139. The great irony of course is that the government needed no help turning people against them. More death squads were active in Chalatenango and more massacres occurred there than in any other region except Morazán, site of the famous El Mozote massacre in December 1981 where over 800 people were killed by the death squads.

81. Ibid, 1.
82. Ibid.
83. Carrigan, Ana. *Salvador Witness: The Life and Calling of Jean Donovan.* New York: Simon and Schuster, 1984, 245, 247. This is the official version of what happened, they left in a van, and were stopped at a road block, then taken to a nearby station for questioning. Father Paul Schindler, who testified at the trial of the Guardsmen, claims that they never got into the van. Parishioners working at the airport claim that the Guardsmen were waiting for them at the airport, and they were taken straight into custody. The van was later disposed of. Ita and Maura were likely the targets, and Jean and Dorothy were taken to leave no witnesses. Probably the women were taken to the National Guard station in Zacatecaluca where they were raped and tortured, then driven up past San Pedro.
84. Interview with Father Paul Schindler, December 2, 2009. To have a vehicle coming up the road at that late hour was so unusual people noticed, and after the National Guard had left some of the locals went out and saw the bodies, but were afraid to call any local authorities. Instead, after seeing the bodies buried, they called the local parish priest, who called the Archbishop. Father Paul was with the first church delegation who came to identify the bodies.
85. Carrigan, 249. Father Paul commented that it was illegal in El Salvador to touch a grave site without official permission. Ambassador White was the United States ambassador and one of the few U.S. dignitaries in the country who actively pursued justice in the case.
86. Carrigan, Ana. *Salvador Witness: The Life and Calling of Jean Donovan.* New York: Simon and Schuster, 1984, 251. Eyewitnesses report that Jean's face was unrecognizable because of the bullet wounds, Jean and Ita were badly bruised all over their bodies, and that the stench of all four bodies was terrible. Today there is a small chapel constructed on the site, and a memorial marker placed where the bodies were found. A mass of memorial is celebrated each year there on December second and the chapel is now used regularly by the local parish. This quote was also caught on tape in the film "Roses in December" a documentary about the events. Because Father Paul Schindler had been giving Interviews to CNN, BBC and other news services, several camera crews came with them to document the events.
87. While Jean Donovan was a member of the Cleveland Team since she met the missionary group while at Case Western, she actually grew up in Connecticut. Father Paul Schindler notes that the Reagan Administration added insult to injury when they sent the Donovan family a $3,500 dollar bill for transporting the body back to the States using a government plane. Interview December 2, 2009.
88. Sobrino, Jon. "El Martirio De Maura, Ita, Dorothy Y Jean." Diakonia 16 (1980): 2.
89. Ibid. "¿Hasta Cuándo, Señor?" "Alegrate Jerusalén, la liberación está cerca."
90. Ibid, 3. "Por esta vez al Cristo que ha muerto han sido cuatro mujeres, religiosas y norteamericanas. Y por ello la negrura del crimen va acompañada de una especial luz ... El Cristo muerte son cuatro mujeres." Italics are Sobrino's emphasis.
91. Ibid, 4. "Las cuatro hermanas se han unido al pueblo salvadoreña al unirse a la mujer salvadoreña. La mujer es creadora de fortaleza, que no abandona al que

sufre, como no abandonaron a su pueblo las cuatro hermanas, a pesar de las serias amenazas."

92. Ibid, 3. "La Iglesia . . . sólo puede agradecerles desde lo más profundo de su corazón."

93. Ibid. "Nuestra última palabra tiene que ser: gracias. Con Maura, Ita, Dorothy, y Jean, Dios pasó por El Salvador."

94. UCA Centro Romero Archives. There is a map in the museum of the Centro Romero which details the location of Salvadoran Army troops in the days leading up to November 16. One can clearly see that members of the infamous Atlacatl Battalion controlled the area around the UCA and were supported by Puma and Jaguar Battalions, also elite troops. More than half of the Atlacatl members were trained at the now infamous School of the Americas at Fort Benning, while the rest were trained by U.S. military advisors in El Salvador. See also Jack Nelson-Pallmayer's *School of Assassins: Guns, Greed, and Globalization*. Maryknoll, New York: Orbis Books, 2001.

95. Joseph E. Mulligan, SJ *The Jesuit Martyrs of El Salvador: Celebrating the Anniversaries*. Baltimore, Maryland: Fortkamp Publishing Company, 1994, 7. Mulligan also utilizes the Jesuit provincial's report at the time, and comments that an eyewitness in the retreat center overheard the soldiers speaking, that they wanted to rid the country of foreigners, and that Ellacuría was the target.

96. Ibid, 11. Espinoza was a graduate of the Externado San José, the Jesuit high school in San Salvador. He was later horrified to learn that the operation would put his former high school rector Segundo Montes in grave danger, and much of the later eyewitness testimony comes from him. Jesuits at the UCA say he has never gotten over the guilt of what occurred that night.

97. Ibid, 12. For a comprehensive analysis of these events see also Whitfield, Teresa. *Paying the Price: Ignacio Ellacuría and the murdered Jesuits of El Salvador*. Philadelphia: Temple University Press, 1994. The information about Segundo Montes was provided on a tour of the Romero Center, the Jesuit Garden, and so forth. which included a pamphlet of explanation. The Jesuits had held a community meeting late that night, but all of the Jesuits were sleeping, except Martin-Baró, a known night owl, who was still fully dressed.

98. The Jesuit housekeeper was staying in a nearby guest house with her husband, and witnessed all of the events of that nights. She went undetected because it was not a house normally used, and the lights were all off since they had been asleep. She would later be questioned for seven consecutive days, when she was intercepted by U.S. government officials in Miami on her way to Spain. She was subjected to as many as four polygraphs per day, some in front of Salvadoran security forces. Her testimony was later thrown out at trial since it was "inconsistent." Lecture at the UCA, Twentieth Anniversary Commemoration, November 15, 2009.

99. Apparently the two women were not mortally wounded, and a soldier riddled them with bullets on his way out when he heard them moaning. The photos show that Elba tried to shield sixteen-year-old Celina's body with her own. The photos also show the tremendous wounds of the women, and the blood loss. In the second round of shooting Elba's face was horribly disfigured. One can see some photos between pages 76 and 77 of Mulligan's book, but copies of the official photos taken by the

police and other Jesuits are kept on file in the Romero Center at the UCA. These graphic photos are not for the faint of heart.

100. López y López was much older than the rest, and was dying of cancer at the time he was killed. There are many accounts of the death of these Jesuits and their collaborators, some with minor inaccuracies. Mulligan, SJ and Martha Doggett, as well as the U.N. Truth commission statements have the most consistent accounts. See Doggett, Martha. *Death Foretold: The Jesuit Murders in El Salvador*. Washington D.C.: Georgetown University Press, 1993.

101. This detail was confirmed in an Interview with Jon Sobrino, SJ on November 27, 2009. The book is now on display at the Romero Center Museum at the UCA. The rest of the bodies were left as they lay, either because the soldiers were afraid, or in response to FMLN troop movements that evening.

102. For copies of the letters, see Diaz, Ruben Murillo, ed. *Noviembre De 1989: El Asesinato De Los Jesuitas En El Salvador*. Mexico City: Universidad Iberoamericana, 1990, 16–18.

103. Mulligan, 17–18. Translation from the Spanish from Mulligan.

104. Ibid, 24. The U.N. Truth Commission would later find Lt. Col. Rivas was involved in the cover-up.

105. Interview with John Giuliano, community organizer in Chalatenango, December 12, 2009. Giuliano said that Cortina would probably never have made it past the roadblocks leaving his small village, and that some of the local leaders knew of the offensive the FMLN had planned in San Salvador so didn't want him to return to the UCA. Undoubtedly he would never have made it past the government roadblocks either. Cortina heard his own name, along with Sobrino's, announced by the right wing radio stations as being among the dead.

106. Interview with Jon Sobrino, November 27, 2009.

107. Sobrino, Jon, ed. *Companions of Jesus: The Jesuit Martyrs of El Salvador*. Maryknoll, New York: Orbis Books, 1990, 6.

108. Ibid, 7–9.

109. Ibid, 43. Interview with Jon Sobrino, SJ November 27, 2009. Sobrino admits that the term Jesuanic may be one that he himself has coined. For Sobrino Jesuanic means that they died like Jesus, by taking up their own crosses and dying for all of humanity, but especially the poor.

110. Berryman, Phillip. *Stubborn Hope: Religion, Politics and Revolution in Central America*. Maryknoll, New York: Orbis Books, 1994, 69. Forensics experts from Argentina who examined the remains estimate the numbers to be much higher but at least 800. When one visits the site today, the museum has a collection of all the bullets, some of which still have the U.S. manufacturers name on them. One eyewitness claims that the torture and killing started before December 11 and actually lasted three days.

Photo of Archbishop Oscar Romero celebrating mass.
Photo courtesy of Biblioteca Oscar Romero, UCA, San Salvador.

Photo of Archbishop Oscar Romero preaching at mass.
Photo courtesy of Biblioteca Oscar Romero, UCA, San Salvador.

Photo of Archbishop Oscar Romero.
Photo courtesy of Biblioteca Oscar Romero,
UCA, San Salvador

Photo of Archbishop Oscar Romero.
Photo courtesy of Biblioteca Oscar Romero, UCA, San Salvador.

Photo of the installation of Oscar Romero as Archbishop of San Salvador, March 1977. Rutilio Grande, SJ, master of ceremonies pictured at far right.
Photo courtesy of Biblioteca Oscar Romero, UCA, San Salvador.

Photo of the grave of Rutilio Grande, SJ, buried alongside Nelson Rutilio Lemus, and Manuel Solarzano at the parish church in El Paisnal, El Salvador.
Photo courtesy of John Thiede, SJ.

Photo of Ignacio Ellacuría, SJ, rector of the Jesuit community killed at the UCA on November 16, 1989.
Photo courtesy of Biblioteca Oscar Romero, UCA, San Salvador.

Photo of Ignacio Ellacuría, SJ, pictured receiving honorary degree at Santa Clara University in 1985.
Photo courtesy of Biblioteca Oscar Romero, UCA, San Salvador.

Photo of Martin Baró, SJ, playing guitar at a small chapel in rural El Salvador.
Photo courtesy of Biblioteca Oscar Romero, UCA, San Salvador.

Photo of Martin Baró, SJ, celebrating mass at a small chapel in rural El Salvador.
Photo courtesy of Biblioteca Oscar Romero, UCA, San Salvador.

Photo of Amando López, SJ, Jesuit priest killed at the UCA on November 16, 1989.
Photo courtesy of Biblioteca Oscar Romero, UCA, San Salvador.

Photo of Amando López, SJ, Jesuit priest killed at the UCA on November 16, 1989.
Photo courtesy of Biblioteca Oscar Romero, UCA, San Salvador.

Photo of Joaquin López y López, SJ, Jesuit priest killed at the UCA on November 16, 1989.
Photo courtesy of Biblioteca Oscar Romero, UCA, San Salvador.

Photo of Segundo Montes, SJ, Jesuit priest killed at the UCA on November 16, 1989.
Photo courtesy of Biblioteca Oscar Romero, UCA, San Salvador

Photo of Segundo Montes (right), SJ, Jesuit priest killed at the UCA on November 16, 1989.

Photo of Celina Ramos, 16 year old girl killed alongside the Jesuits at the UCA on November 16, 1989.
Photo courtesy of Biblioteca Oscar Romero, UCA, San Salvador.

Photo of Elba Ramos, cook at the Jesuit theologate killed at the UCA on November 16, 1989.
Photo courtesy of Biblioteca Oscar Romero, UCA, San Salvador.

Documentation photo of Jesuits killed on the back lawn of the Jesuit community at the UCA on November 16, 1989.
Photo courtesy of Biblioteca Oscar Romero, UCA, San Salvador.

Photo of the tomb of the Jesuits killed on November 16, 1989 at the UCA university chapel.
Photo courtesy of John Thiede, SJ.

Photo of Jon Sobrino, SJ, Jesuit priest lecturing at the UCA university chapel on the occasion of the 20th anniversary of the UCA martyrs.
Photo courtesy of John Thiede, SJ.

Chapter Five

Martyrdom in *Christology at the Crossroads* (pre-1989)

Johann Baptist Metz suggests in his work *Faith in History in Society* that it is nearly impossible for a theologian to do theology in a vacuum, ignoring the world outside.[1] Since liberation theology blossoms forth from the Latin American context, and Sobrino's Christology is contextual and rooted in the Central and Latin American context, then the events examined in the previous chapter must impact in some way the person of Jon Sobrino, and his Christology. While one could question the scope of the impact of the outside world on Sobrino's Christology, certainly the war in El Salvador shapes it. But one could argue that the events of 1989, the massacre of the Jesuit community at the UCA and their two collaborators forever changed Sobrino. In fact, this argument will serve as the starting point of this chapter. When examining Sobrino's Christology and the reality of martyrdom, the events of 1989 form a pivotal point for a sharpening of his Christology and a broadening of his view of martyrdom. This is not to say that the assassination of Romero, the deaths of the U.S. churchwomen or the murder of Rutilio Grande on the road to El Paisnal did not affect Sobrino as well, but they did not impact him with the same force as the massacre of his own community.[2] While the civil war disrupted the lives of Sobrino and all Salvadorans, not all events shaped him with the same weight, nor in the same way. So if we presume 1989 and the massacre at the UCA as a pivotal point for Sobrino, we have a dividing date for Sobrino's work concerning martyrdom.

This chapter will examine the key aspects of Sobrino's Christology before 1989. After a brief discussion of his methodological reasons for emphasizing the historical Jesus, three points will be used as a framework from which to build and expand upon for Sobrino's work after 1989. First, the term martyr, while used before 1989, will be expanded later to coin a new term, Jesuanic martyr. Second, the cross, ever present in Sobrino's Christology will be expanded later and applied to Ellacuría's ideas concerning the crucified peoples. Third, Sobrino makes the claim that discipleship and praxis are the key to following Jesus and announcing the kingdom of God. This idea of discipleship will be deepened and the importance of praxis intensified in Sobrino's later work. When Sobrino departed for El Salvador from Spain in 1957, he probably never envisioned that people he knew, admired and even lived with would become martyrs for the kingdom. But he would live this reality and his Christology would be irreversibly shaped by it.

AN INTELLECTUAL BIOGRAPHY OF JON SOBRINO

If one examines Sobrino's early theological work, at first glance one is hard pressed to find a plethora of references to martyrdom. As we saw in previous chapters, the revolutions which began in Mexico before 1950, and in South America beginning in the 1960s, did not hit full stride in Central America until the 1970s. Sobrino arrived in El Salvador for the first time in 1957 as a Jesuit novice, with the intention of being a missionary and spending the rest of his life there.[3] Ernesto Valiente observes,

> Like many other missionaries prior to him, the young Sobrino arrived in Central America not so much with the intention of encountering and engaging a new world, but rather intent on expanding his own. In a recent reflection on these years the theologian recalls that at the time he understood his mission as one to "help the Salvadorans replace their popular 'superstitious' religiosity with a more sophisticated kind, and . . . help the Latin American branches of the church (the European church) to grow."[4]

After the novitiate and juniorate Sobrino was sent to the U.S. for philosophy studies in St. Louis. Later he admits that this stage of largely Thomistic formation in the heart of the Missouri Valley would not adequately prepare him for ministry in El Salvador.[5] The problem for the Jesuits in El Salvador at the time was that they did not have an adequate place for philosophical and theological formation, so the Jesuit scholastics were sent abroad for their training. Sobrino was sent to St. Louis with the hope that he would have a solid philosophical formation, learn English, and also study engineering so he might one day teach at the Jesuit University in San Salvador, the UCA. When Sobrino returned to San Salvador he taught math and philosophy as a Jesuit regent, at the Jesuit high school.[6]

After regency, Sobrino began his theology training which ended typically in ordination for priesthood. In this case, Sobrino was sent to Frankfurt to study at the Hochschule Sankt Georgen. Sobrino excelled in his studies, so after his ordination he stayed for a doctorate which he finished in 1974. His initial course of studies in Frankfurt were largely dogmatic, but in his PhD dissertation he worked extensively with modern German theologians such as Pannenberg and Moltmann.[7] While certainly his dissertation work proved helpful in the future, so too did insights which came out of the recently ended Second Vatican Council. Valiente writes, "Sobrino's theological understanding began to move away from a positivist study of dogmatic formulas to one more contextualized by historical reality."[8] For Sobrino, as well as other Latin American theologians, Vatican II served as a new light and allowed some theologians to focus more on the reality of Latin America, and less on more esoteric theological works which found little or no application in a world of poverty and suffering. The writings of Pannenberg and Moltmann helped him to move away from more dogmatic concepts and focus more directly on the historical reality of Jesus of Nazareth. In Sobrino's own words, "I discovered that Christ is none other than Jesus and that he conceived a utopia on which all too few have focused: the idea of the kingdom of God."[9]

Sobrino credits Rahner for the most lasting impression during his days of theological training in Germany. In fact, Rahner's ideas about the mystery of God stuck with him through the civil war and perhaps even today.[10] But when he worked on his thesis the idea of differentiating the dogmatic ideas concerning Christ from the more concrete discovery of the historical Jesus of Nazareth started to take shape. It was not that he disagreed with Teilhard de Chardin concerning the "omega point of evolution" or with Rahner with his Christ as "absolute savior." But when he worked on his thesis the idea of differentiating the dogmatic ideas concerning Christ from the more concrete discovery of the historical Jesus of Nazareth started to take shape.

Sobrino also reflects on the fact that the reality around him forced him to confront his dogmatic slumber. He mentions Ignacio Ellacuría and Monseñor Romero as examples of Salvadorans and martyrs who help him awaken. He writes, "In this situation, I had the chance to encounter others who had already woken from the sleep of inhumanity: Ignacio Ellacuría and, later Monsignor Romero, to name two great Salvadorans, Christians, and martyrs, great brothers and friends."[11] These martyrs also led him to greater encounters with the poor and the marginalized in his adopted Salvadoran homeland. He describes this awakening as one which forever alters his life, and radically changes his questions about the world and how theology might respond to it. Certainly this time period must have been confusing for Sobrino, since it became a kind of paradigm shift or in his words "the headscratcher that is human life."[12] This turning of the world upside down was also an enjoyable process for Sobrino. He describes the process as a better way to live, to enjoy life with greater joy and with greater meaning. It allowed him to write with a new perspective looking back on the previous years of his life. These new eyes allowed him to see both the good and the bad: massacres, terrible poverty, injustice, but also hope, creativity and generosity. Both the darkness and the light lead to a discovery and revelation of the truth of reality, the truth of humanity, and the truth of God.[13]

SOBRINO'S EARLY CHRISTOLOGY: MARTYRDOM, CROSS, DISCIPLESHIP, AND KINGDOM OF GOD

In *Christology at the Crossroads*, one does not find many references to martyrdom. In part, that is because in this first work, he is still influenced by European theology and his theological formation, but also because he has not found a way to adapt this theology to the reality he finds in El Salvador. That is not to say that martyrdom is not important for Sobrino's early Christology. It is just not as present as it will be in his later works and writings. In the book, Sobrino wants to introduce the idea of praxis and the integral part it should play in Christian life. In addition, Sobrino claims that one cannot have a Christology without including the historical person of Jesus of Nazareth. Even in his early work he is adamant about stressing the humanity of Jesus in part as a counter balance to a Salvadoran church that in the past overly stressed the divinity of Jesus. Some basic tenets of liberation theology act as a correction to a very cerebral or a Christological view of Jesus Christ from above. Working against those who portray Jesus as divinely distant, Sobrino promoted the idea of the kingdom of God present here in this world, at this time. This of course comes directly out of the Vatican II document *Lumen Gentium*. A concrete historical person, Jesus of Nazareth comes into the world to announce that the kingdom of God is here, real and at hand. Jesus then "proclaims the coming utopia; he denounces injustice as the epitome of sin; he shows partiality towards the oppressed; he unmasks alienating religious mechanisms."[14] The Spirit of Jesus also plays an integral role in insuring the kingdom of God. Sobrino advocates a Spirit of Jesus intimately involved in Christian praxis.

Sobrino admits that this Christology shifts our focus to a new understanding of Jesus which is praxis based. When Jesus proclaims the coming of the Kingdom of God, he also denounces injustice. The hope is to realize the kingdom "in real life" which in turn will lead us to a new kind of discipleship.[15] The first chapter of the book intimately ties the historical Jesus to Christian praxis. During the 1970s the church in El Salvador entered a period of profound ecclesiological crisis especially with respect to actively living the faith. Sobrino does not object to the creedal statements nor the formulas advanced at the Council of Chalcedon but does want to begin from a different starting point using "a biblical focus on Christ" and making the effort to discover "the distinctive character of Christ's person—his divine Sonship."[16] This approach will examine the divine titles used for Jesus in the Bible which are properly attributed to Christ, but only after first reflecting upon the major events from the life of Jesus. Starting with the historical Jesus avoids the tendency towards abstractionism as well as a manipulation of the events from the life of Christ. With the historical Jesus as the hermeneutical principle, Sobrino draws the reader into the totality of the life of Christ in both knowledge and real life praxis.

This focus on the historical Jesus as a starting point draws on a new Latin American approach which arises out of concrete experience and faith practice. Sobrino writes, "The historical Jesus would serve as a satisfactory midway point between two extremes: turning Christ into an abstraction on the one hand, or putting him to direct and immediate ideological uses on the other."[17] Sobrino wants to avoid both extremes, similar to Gustavo Gutiérrez and Ignacio Ellacuría who also avoid the extremes of these two poles. But Sobrino does more than just appeal to Latin American theologians to justify his starting point. He sees in the world around him a similarity to the world of the historical Jesus. Poverty and exploitation plagued the world of Jesus, just as they did in the El Salvador of the 1970s, 1980s and 1990s. Latin American Christology hopes to resolve some of the same issues as the early Christian community.

THE CROSS

As mentioned at the beginning of the chapter, it will be instructive to highlight three different areas in Sobrino's *Christology at the Crossroads*—cross, discipleship and the proclamation of the kingdom of God. Of particular interest will be where martyrdom fits into this particular liberation Christology. Before moving to Sobrino's ideas regarding the cross, it might be helpful to remember the Ignatian meditation on the Cross from the Spiritual Exercises since the Exercises were an integral part of Sobrino's Jesuit formation and influence his thinking about the cross. The meditation on the cross falls in the third week of the Exercises.[18] After meditating on the passion narratives, including the agony in the garden, and the sentencing by Pilate, the exercitant is asked to meditate on Jesus being raised on the cross and the death of Jesus. This meditation is important enough for Ignatius to suggest two repetitions, or three prayer periods total plus an evening application of the senses. In annotation 297 Ignatius suggests that all four gospel accounts may be used, with special emphasis on the two thieves, recommending St. John to his mother, the thirst of Jesus, Jesus giving up his spirit, the division of his garments and the thrust of the lance which pours forth water and blood. The exercitant then spends an entire day contemplating the burial of Jesus, the grief and fatigue of Mary, and the loneliness of the disciples. The Exercises are important because the cross was likely an annual contemplation for Sobrino, and the power which the cross holds likely goes beyond just an intellectual one. In addition, Sobrino mentions these Ignatian influences in his appendix, in particular the Ignatian emphasis on the Kingdom of God, and the "praxis oriented nature of the Exercises."[19] In many ways Sobrino's contemplation on the cross enriches his Christology. His Ignatian imagination allows him to go beyond the stock theological view of the cross, seen especially when he broadens the cross of Jesus to include the poor and the oppressed. Sobrino sees the Ignatian meditations as being grounded in the historical Jesus and the second and third weeks as being essential to this understanding.[20]

The appendix of the book is crucial because it expresses Sobrino's outlook on the cross. The Salvadoran war could be considered a "third week" experience. With nightly roundups and killings by death squads, and with children, parents and grandparents among the "disappeared" one could pick any of the myriad of scriptural passages during Jesus' Passion, Resurrection and Death to meditate upon. Certainly in various retreats throughout his Jesuit life Sobrino actively prayed through these passages. Furthermore his images for a crucified people cannot be denied. The cross has been a theme for Sobrino since the time of his dissertation. His dissertation thesis relies heavily on Moltmann's ideas concerning the cross, especially the idea of the Crucified God. In Sobrino's own words, "Moltmann moved from the God of the future to the crucified God, from anticipatory recollection of Christ's resurrection to the perilous memory of the crucified Jesus, from hope in Christ's future to the following of the historical Jesus."[21] Moltmann provides a political theology of the cross which in terms of theodicy, reconciles God with evil, sin, injustice, death and responds to the cry of suffering in the world. The key concept combines the cross with the Risen Jesus or what Moltmann describes as the cross of the risen one. It is because of the cross that Moltmann defines God as the "crucified God" and constructs a Christology and a theology "on the basis of Jesus's cross."[22]

Sobrino also ties the death of Jesus on the cross to the idea of liberation. He asserts that Jesus of Nazareth, Jesus the Christ, Son of God died by crucifixion. From the very beginning the cross becomes a kind of "dividing line between Christian existence and every other type of religion."[23] Sometimes theologians sidestep the task of reflecting on the cross itself. While some theologians might reflect on being saved by the cross of Jesus, many end by "eliminating the element of scandal in the historical cross of Jesus."[24] In

Latin America the cross has often been a main focus in popular religiosity. In general, the main focus of the Triduum is on Good Friday and not Easter Sunday. But one could seek a more activist interpretation of the cross. Sobrino contends, "While the resurrection remains the paradigm of liberation, the cross is no longer seen simply as a symbol of suffering or as the negative dialectical moment which immediately and directly gives rise to the positive moment of liberation."[25] One must engage the cross in order to experience the liberating force of the resurrection.

This rules out any romantic notions of the cross, often found in the resurrection centered focus of the Easter celebrations in mainstream U.S. culture. Sobrino claims, "The utopia of Christian resurrection becomes real only in terms of the cross, and theological reflection on the death of Jesus must probe deeper on at least two levels."[26] He explains these two levels as the theological level in the strict sense and the suppositions and implications of this particular conception for Christian life. On the one hand, if reflection on the cross does not reach the theological level of asking questions about God and stays simply with the death of Jesus; such reflection ignores the issue at the deepest level. On the other hand, if we ignore the implications of the cross in our present context, we deny the cross in our daily Christian praxis. Two main obstacles preclude: "any attempt to grasp the cross of Jesus in all its profundity. One is the danger of isolating the cross from the concrete history of Jesus; the other is isolating it from God."[27]

RELATIONSHIP TO MARTYRDOM

The theology of the cross also presents three important stages which are relevant to the discussion of what it means to be a martyr in the twenty-first century. First, there is sometimes a skewed emphasis on the positive benefits of the cross for humankind, that is, an overemphasis on the salvific and soteriological aspects of the cross. Secondly, one can recover "a pristine value of the cross" especially by considering the historical outcome and consequence of the lifelong journey of Jesus on the cross which bears witness and challenges the truth of "other religious and political gods."[28] The third, or most radical stage is the consideration of the presence (or absence) of God on the cross of Jesus. Here Moltmann sees the opportunity for a decision: either the cross of Jesus is the end of all Christian theology or it is the beginning of a truly Christian theology that combines critical reflection with a liberative praxis.

In the first stage, Sobrino wants to focus on a post-resurrection view, but one which takes seriously the death of Jesus on the cross. This does not mean he negates Jesus's divinity as the Son of God. Quite the contrary, New Testament divine titles are rescued, and many years later this ideal is developed even further in his book, *Christ the Liberator*. Sobrino questions those who seemingly ignore the cross, ignore the historical Jesus and in doing so "overlook the import of the cross."[29] In addition, too much emphasis on the saving power of the cross leads to a meditation on the mystery of the cross and omits the scandal. Maintaining the scandal of the cross helps impel a person out of a sedentary faith life, and "does not simply ask how people are saved passively; it also asks how God saves people in a world where there is no salvation."[30] By accepting this premise, one must acknowledge the difficulties and not abandon the idea of a crucified God in the history of the church and of theology. For many the acceptance that the Son of God died in scandal, or in disaster, proves difficult. Nevertheless, it is imperative.

Thinking about a God who remains passive during Jesus's death on the cross can also prove disconcerting. It is much easier to imagine God as omnipotent and all-powerful. This emphasis on the scandal provides a counterpoint to a more Anselmian theory of vicarious satisfaction or the classic medieval interpretation of the salvific meaning of the death of Jesus. In Anselm's model the infinite distance between the Father and creation is healed by the Son, and "due reparation is made to the Father through the cross of his Son, and thus the sins of humankind are forgiven."[31] Sobrino reads the ultimate flaw in this viewpoint as ahistorical. The cross is interpreted in terms of God's overall design and never enters the historical reality of Jesus and his cross. This view welcomes a God who suffers alongside humanity. One hears echoes of Bonhoeffer's phrase "Only a God who suffers can save us," imagines Moltmann's idea that a God who suffers is also a God who loves, and realizes that "An inability to suffer would contradict the basic Christian assertion that God is love."[32] In the end the point is fairly simple: "the man, Jesus of Nazareth, who died a failure on the cross and abandoned by God, is really and truly the Son of God."[33] This paradox of the scandal of the cross cannot be ignored. The locus is not only the resurrection but also the cross of Jesus.

Admittedly, this focus on the cross leads to more focus on the humanity of Jesus and the incarnation. Instead of placing the emphasis on Jesus surpassing his own humanity, Sobrino wants God's plan to be understood in terms of "the real, authentic incarnation of God."[34] This does not mean that the cross is simply the end of ministry for Jesus, but rather shows Jesus as a faithful witness to the coming of the Kingdom of God here on earth. This announcement of the kingdom in the face of the Jewish establishment necessarily introduces conflict into the heart of the life of Jesus. Accepting the incarnation, his own flesh and blood, causes Jesus to either choose to confront the establishment or watch passively. Sobrino shows that Jesus confronts the realities working against the reign of God, and that "Jesus's polemics with the religious authorities were not just a didactic exercise; they flowed naturally from the inner dynamism of the incarnation."[35] By making God present, by making the claim that God's grace is accessible to all people and goes beyond any legalistic ritualism, Jesus meets a tragic end on the cross. The triumph of the cross then, can be seen as a triumph of the announcement of the kingdom as a kingdom for everyone, and a realization that God's grace can be accessed by all people regardless of social standing, culture, or economic prowess.

DISCIPLESHIP

Jesus becomes word incarnate in a concrete social situation. This concrete situation entails suffering and in the end death on the cross. The summons to discipleship leads to this concrete end, and reflection on this discipleship helps form a spirituality of the cross. Sobrino claims that this discipleship leads us to a political theology, one which can't be dissociated from the cross. Therefore "identification with the crucified must take place on the way to the cross."[36] When straying from that path, the spirituality of the cross becomes something else, a stoicism, a masochism, a docetism or something completely dissociated with an incarnational view of the cross. Sobrino sees the cross as "the end of the process. If we do not go through that process, then the cross to which we offer our acceptance may not be the Christian cross."[37] Sobrino realizes that this process necessitates a conversion, and following the cross as a disciple of Jesus may lead to a bumpy road at the least, and possibly a conflictual path in countries with an atheistic government, or one which perpetuates suffering in choosing policies which are at odds with the reign of God.

The end of the cross section in this chapter of *Christology at the Crossroads* describes one of the most significant expositions of how martyrdom might potentially befall a person who faithfully follows Jesus and the cross. This is the only significant treatment of the theme of martyrdom in the book, and the first time it is mentioned. Sobrino begins by acknowledging that "there have been many martyrs for religious and political reasons, both before and after Jesus's time."[38] There have been martyrs for political and religious reasons before and after the time of Jesus. While Jesus was also a prophet, there was nothing beautiful about his death, nor was he just another martyr. But the death of Jesus "differed from that of other martyrs and prophets for they died with the intention that their death should serve as their last act in defense of their cause. Thus their death often stood in continuity with their life and their cause . . . By contrast Jesus dies in total discontinuity with his life and his cause. The death he experienced was not only the death of his person but also the death of his cause."[39]

Sobrino claims that the martyrdom of Jesus is distinctive due to three key elements: his message concerning the imminent approach of God, his cry on the cross, and his abandonment by the Father. For this last point, one can identify a strong reliance on Moltmann and his ideas on the crucified Jesus abandoned by God the Father on the cross. Acknowledging this abandonment allows a person to experience the history of injustice and oppression and also "hear the cry of Jesus on the cross and the cry of countless victims in history."[40] But for the first two points, one can see Sobrino's own Christology beginning to shine forth, especially when he writes about Jesus announcing the reign of God and following Jesus in discipleship in a Latin American context.

Sobrino ends his chapters related to the cross by affirming that the resurrection of Jesus should always be viewed in connection with the cross. Following Jesus leads toward a life of faith, hope and love. Christian faith is not independent of all of the groans and cries throughout history and viewed in the light of the cross takes shape by attacking unbelief. Christian hope is not a pure optimism but one which is rooted "in a hope *against* injustice, oppression and death."[41] The cross of Jesus does not defeat hope but rather gives hope to those who are crucified today in real historical contexts. The cross of Christ gives Christian love a different dimension, a love which goes to the extreme. This love is not idealistic, nor simply pragmatic but the ultimate word uttered on the cross or in John's Gospel: "There is no greater love that this—to lay down one's life for one's friends"(John 15:13). Faith, hope and love consummate in the final end on the cross. These virtues are what make the cross and resurrection our central faith components. The scandal of the cross gives us a reality that is open to the world, forcing us to change our way of thinking, and moves us to enter into real history. The cross is not alienating, instead it calls our life into question and "makes it possible for history to keep moving forward toward the kingdom of God in hope and love."[42]

KINGDOM OF GOD

Sobrino often relates his ideas concerning martyrdom with the idea that Jesus is always at the service of God's kingdom. This means that Jesus is not the primary focus of his preaching, but rather the central focus is the kingdom of God. Jesus did not simply talk about God; he spoke about the kingdom of God. Clearly "in historical terms we can only come to know the historical Jesus in and through the notion of God's kingdom. By the same token we can only come to understand what is meant by the kingdom of God in and through Jesus."[43] Jesus's utilization of the term "kingdom of God" is nothing novel.

The term appears frequently in the Hebrew Scriptures and suggests two basic notions: "(1) God reigns with acts of power, (2) in order to establish or modify the order of things."[44] But Jesus appeals to the apocalyptic thinking of his time period when speaking about the definitive reign of God which people are awaiting. Jesus affirms that God exists and the reign of God is at hand. This reign also implies that all people are both oriented toward God while also enjoying fellowship as brothers and sisters. This affirmation has greater implications. Therefore "the mere verbal proclamation of God without action to achieve his reign is not enough and orthopraxis must take priority over orthodoxy."[45] In this way it is not simply enough to proclaim that God exists. For Jesus proclaiming God also necessitates the realization of the reign of God in practice.

Jesus acknowledges that God's grace surrounds us and that the kingdom of God is already at hand. But Jesus does not simply preach—the in-breaking of the Kingdom also finds its expression in deeds. The actions of Jesus "are not simply accompaniment to his words, nor are they primarily designed to illustrate his own person. Their primary value is theo-logical: They are meant to demonstrate the kingdom of God."[46] The actions of Jesus demonstrate that the reign of God is at hand. For this reason preaching and practice cannot be separated; both lead to liberation for Sobrino. Sobrino shows that the form in which Jesus preaches and acts takes the form of liberation. He doesn't just preach about God's kingdom, but he also heals the sick, touches lepers, talks to a Samaritan woman, associates with the Roman centurion, a foreigner, etc. By eating meals with both friends and sinners Jesus welcomes this eschatological reality. Sobrino also disputes a more traditional interpretation of miracles and the forgiveness of sins as solely manifesting the divinity of Jesus. This interpretation denies the importance of the reign of God announced by Jesus. Instead, "Both his miracles and his forgiveness of sins are primary signs of the arrival of the kingdom of God. They are signs of liberation, and only in that context can they help to shed light on the person of Jesus."[47] Jesus performing miracles and forgiving sins announces the coming kingdom. As Christians, a relationship with Jesus signifies a relational character with others and assumes an attitude of service to the Kingdom of God. In this way a relationship with Jesus will not be fully realized "through cultic acclamation or adoration but through following Jesus in the service of God's kingdom."[48]

A more robust understanding of sin orients a person of faith toward the kingdom of God. When Jesus preaches the good news in a sinful world he points us toward liberation. Jesus also viewed sins as a burden which must be alleviated. Sobrino writes, "Sin is not just something that must be pardoned. It must be taken away, eradicated."[49] If sin is the rejection of God's kingdom here on earth, and if a Christian does not allow grace to fully enter his or her heart, in the end it is not only a rejection of God but in turn power and social sin can also lead to oppressing others. One can understand sin in two different dimensions, the personal and the social. Sobrino states, "The personal dimension was a refusal to accept the future of the God who was approaching in grace. The social dimension was a refusal to anticipate that future reality in our here-and-now life . . . Sin is no longer seen as directed against God but rather against the kingdom of God."[50]

For this reason, the proclamation of the kingdom of God necessitates conversion. Conversion consists of the coming together of grace and works, the fusion of orthodoxy and orthopraxis. The call of the kingdom is a call to discipleship. Just like the first twelve disciples the call puts a person of faith at the disposal of the kingdom. The following of Jesus manifests itself in concrete applications. Faith put into practice signifies "a concrete obligation to fight for love and justice among human beings."[51] This fight is not chosen arbitrarily by Jesus. In the revelation of the kingdom, Jesus reveals a meaningful future for those living in oppression, hope for the hopeless. It also obliges one to take up one's own cross and follow Jesus as a disciple. In sum, one cannot divorce the historical Jesus from the announcement of the reign of God.

This section has developed three major ideas in Sobrino's Christology; the praxis of faith through discipleship which helps the committed Christian to participate in the announcement of the reign of God, and the central focus on the cross. But in terms of a systematic development of how martyrdom fits into Sobrino's Christology or even a working definition of the term martyr one might be left unsatisfied, since very little has been mentioned thus far. Sobrino does utilize the term martyr when referring to Rutilio Grande and Oscar Romero but does not write extensively on the topic, other than a brief essay in the 1983 Concilium edition *Martyrdom Today* where he suggests, along with Rahner and Metz, that perhaps the current thinking on what it means to be a martyr could be revisited.[52] He does devote a brief section on the cross to what it means to be a martyr and also writes briefly about martyrdom in a 1981 article later published in a collection of essays in English in 1987.[53] Here he describes the greatest surrender of discipleship—martyrdom. Sobrino writes, "Surrender to Jesus in discipleship during life attains its greatest depth of surrender in death and in that death that is particularly Christian: martyrdom."[54] In this article Sobrino describes a Christology of liberation. He sees martyrdom as testifying to the hope in Jesus. Martyrdom is a praxic form of discipleship and a response to the call to follow Christ.

Other than the brief mention of martyrdom in *Christology at the Crossroads*, the Concilium article and the passing mention in this 1981 essay, martyrdom is not significantly mentioned in Sobrino's work before 1989.

But after 1989, following the assassination of members of his Jesuit community and their coworkers, Sobrino increasingly elaborates on the topic and develops new ideas with greater depth and conviction. Examining the reality around him makes Sobrino rethink what it means to be a martyr and to coin a new term "Jesuanic martyr." If one were to ask the question: Is there a dialectical relationship between Sobrino's Christology and martyrdom before 1989? The answer would be no. But after 1989 the answer is yes: martyrdom weaves its way into his Christology, impacting it, and causing him to broaden the categories of discipleship, cross, the kingdom of God, and what it means to be a martyr today.

NOTES

1. One can see this especially in the fourth and fifth chapter of this work, perhaps exemplified in the quote: "The church must understand itself and prove itself as the public witness and bearer of a dangerous memory of freedom in the 'systems' of our emancipatory society." Johann Baptist Metz. *Faith in History and Society: Toward a Practical Fundamental Theology.* Translated by J. Matthew Ashley. New York: The Crossroad Publishing Co., 2007, 88.

2. One might also say that all of these events had a cumulative effect culminating in the events of 1989 for Sobrino.

3. Sobrino was actually born in Barcelona in 1938, the product of Basque parents who were living in the Catalan capital at the time.

4. Orfilio Ernesto Valiente. "Truth, Justice, and Forgiveness: Reconciliation in Jon Sobrino's Christology" Dissertation, University of Notre Dame, 2010, 87. He quotes Sobrino from Principle of Mercy, 2.

5. See chapter one, "Awakening from a Dogmatic Slumber" in Sobrino, Jon. *The Principle of Mercy: Taking the Crucified People from the Cross.* Maryknoll, NY: Orbis Books, 1994, one of his most autobiographical essays. See also Ernesto Valiente's dissertation which sets a nice time frame for his theological work especially when he traces Sobrino's intellectual biography from pages 97 to 105.

6. Jesuit regency then, as now, usually consisted of two to three years of teaching in a Jesuit high school, in this case, the Externado in San Salvador, which still stands today. Interview with Salvador Carranza, Externado San Javier, San Salvador, December 2009.

7. Valiente Dissertation, 90. Valiente notes that Sobrino's dissertation was titled Le Dieu Crucifié (on the crucified God) and offers a critique of the Christologies of Jurgen Moltmann and Wolfhart Pannenberg, in footnote 40.

8. Ibid.

9. Sobrino, "Introduction: Awakening from the Sleep of Inhumanity," 2. The original version of this work was actually written in English in 1991 and later translated into Spanish. The Spanish title of the essay is "Introducción: Despertar del sueño de la cruel inhumanidad."

10. Sobrino, *Despertar del Sueño*, 13 . . . "La teología de Rahner—por poner el ejemplo mas beneficioso para mí—me acompaño durante aquellos años, y sus páginas sobre el misterio de Dios siguen acompañandome hasta hoy." This first edition translation which Sobrino wrote originally in Spanish was published in 1992.

11. Ibid, 15. "En esa situación, tuve la dicha de encontrarme con otros que ya habían depertado del sueño de la inhumanidad: Ignacio Ellacuría y, después Monseñor Romero, por citar a dos grandes salvadoreños, cristianos y mártires, grandes hermanos y amigos."

12. Ibid. This process of headscratching or "rompecabezas," literally head breaking, alternate translation puzzle solving, changes the order of the moveable parts of different problems. Different questions lead to different methodologies, and different problematics.

13. Ibid, 16. "Pero lo que quiero mencionar ahora es el redescubrimiento que es anterior a todo esto: la revelación de la verdad de la realidad y, a través de ella, de la verdad de los seres humanos y de la verdad de Dios."

14. Sobrino, *Christology at the Crossroads*, xxv.

15. Ibid. To put the timing of this book in perspective, the Spanish version was already released before the death of Rutilio Grande, SJ in 1977.

16. Ibid, 5.

17. Ibid, 10.

18. David Fleming, ed. *The Spiritual Exercises of St. Ignatius*. St. Louis: The Institute of Jesuit Sources, 1978. See especially annotations 190–209.

19. Sobrino, *Christology at the Crossroads*, 399. Sobrino also notes the importance of discipleship and following Jesus, which stem from the second week of the Exercises. For more on the Christ of the Exercises see his appendix pp. 396–424.

20. Ibid, 413. Sobrino outlines the schematic of the exercises as God-Christ-God. The first and the fourth weeks corresponding to God, and the second and third weeks corresponding to Jesus Christ. He ties in the cross, discipleship and the Kingdom of God especially to the second and third weeks in this appendix.

21. Ibid, 29. One can see the implications for discipleship here as well, following the same Jesus of history who is crucified on the cross.

22. Ibid, 32.

23. Ibid, 179.

24. Ibid, 180.

25. Ibid.

26. Ibid, 181.

27. Ibid.

28. Ibid, 181–82.

29. Ibid, 184. While Sobrino does think that an overemphasis of the divine or honorific titles for Jesus can lead to a de-emphasis of his life here on earth, he does not want to abandon these titles.

30. Ibid, 190.

31. Ibid, 192.

32. Ibid, 197.

33. Ibid, 200.

34. Ibid, 202. According to Sobrino, this again works against a viewpoint more like Anselm which speaks of Jesus's crucifixion solely as a work of redemption.
35. Ibid, 207.
36. Ibid, 216.
37. Ibid, 217.
38. Ibid, 218. In fact, the index of the book does not even have martyrdom as a sub-heading, whereas martyrdom is listed in Sobrino's two major Christological works published after 1989.
39. Ibid.
40. Ibid, 231.
41. Ibid, 232. Italics author's emphasis.
42. Ibid, 235.
43. Ibid, 41. Sobrino admits he is not the only theologian who emphasizes this fact, noting that Rahner himself taught this.
44. Ibid, 43. Other Latin American theologians write on this same topic, notably Leonardo Boff and his ideas concerning utopia.
45. Ibid, 45.
46. Ibid, 46–47. One is also reminded of the influence of the Spiritual Exercises of Ignatius here, "Preach the Gospel, when necessary, use words." Some scholars argue that Ignatius borrowed this idea from St. Francis.
47. Ibid, 48.
48. Ibid, 50.
49. Ibid, 51.
50. Ibid, 53.
51. Ibid, 59.
52. Since I discussed this work extensively in the second chapter I will not revisit the essay here. Suffice it to say that in this article Sobrino simply plants the seeds in this five to six page essay for his later work on martyrdom and a potential relationship to his Christology.
53. The original was published in Sobrino, Jon. *Jesús en América Latina* (Santander, Spain: Sal Terrae; San Salvador, El Salvador: Universidad Centroamericana, 1982). The English version is Sobrino, Jon. Chapter One. "The Truth about Jesus Christ" in *Jesus in Latin America*. (Maryknoll, NY: Orbis Books, 1987). p. 28–29 discuss martyrdom.
54. *Jesús en América Latina*, 28.

Chapter Six

Martyrdom in *Jesus the Liberator/Christ the Liberator* (post-1989)

JESUS THE LIBERATOR: CHALLENGE TO A NARROW DEFINITION OF MARTYRDOM

Earlier chapters outlined the development of the meaning of martyrdom in the traditional sense and why there is need for a new or expanded definition. After acknowledging the history of a larger reality in Latin America, the particular case of El Salvador was examined and showed how the political turmoil there produced four exemplary cases of martyrdom for Sobrino. Sobrino's Christological work before 1989 manifests a few influences of these martyrs, but nothing codified or well defined. It is now possible to examine Sobrino's work from 1989 to the present. Sobrino further develops key Christological categories after 1989, especially discipleship and the cross. In addition, the meaning of the word martyr gains a greater theological weight for Sobrino as he coins a new term—the Jesuanic martyr. Martyrdom can be used as a lens with which to understand Sobrino's Christology and responds to Rahner's push for an expanded concept of martyrdom. First, Sobrino expands martyrdom beyond the traditional definition, and by coining a new term, Jesuanic martyr, helps move toward a working definition that may prove helpful for our twenty-first century context. Second, the reality of martyrdom influences Sobrino's Christology, and the new term Jesuanic martyr proves to be a key lens for interpreting his later Christology.

Sobrino's ideas concerning martyrdom evolved over time and can be illustrated by examining two of his key theological works *Jesus the Liberator: A Historical Theological View* and *Christ the Liberator: A View from the Victims.*[1] *Jesus the Liberator* was released in 1993 two years after the original Spanish version in 1991. The book is dedicated to the memory of the six

Jesuits and Elba and Celina Ramos killed at the UCA. The introduction proves telling in that Sobrino answers why he chooses to write another book on Christology. One might think that this book is intended as a sequel to *Christology at the Crossroads*, but in fact it is an updated Christology which builds upon the first and is intended as a two-part series with *Christ the Liberator* which will be finished a decade later. Sobrino admits that writing a new Christology does not come without personal challenges even when writing about a liberating Christ. But Sobrino claims that years after writing his *Christology at the Crossroads* the person of Jesus Christ still speaks to the masses. In this Latin American context he sees a universal Christ but also advances the notion that both Christ and the continent are crucified. He writes, "The relatively pacific 'who do you say that I am?' becomes a pressing question in the mouth of the crucified Christ and the crucified people."[2] Christ can also be grasped as good news too, not just as Christ crucified.

Sobrino acknowledges the significance the reality of El Salvador and the martyrs play in his context for writing this book. He asserts, "The gospel's finest and most original phrases—often taken for granted in Christologies—resound here with real power, as something real. It is a fact that there are crucified peoples, 'flogged Christs,' and this give a better understanding of Christ, the Suffering Servant of Yahweh, hidden among the poor."[3] The innumerable martyrs are still present and active, and the UCA Jesuits, the U.S. churchwomen, Rutilio Grande and Romero help us better understand the martyr Jesus. These many witnesses and martyrs illuminate the witness of Jesus and provide us hope. The challenge of the Salvadoran reality "does not render christology superfluous, but makes it all the more necessary to put all one's intellect into elaborating a christology that will help the resurrection of the Salvadorean people."[4] Hopefully the person of Jesus Christ is united with a concrete reality and experienced as a living faith, not just a theological concept. The good news can be found in the liberator Jesus Christ. Sobrino's intent for this book is also made clear when he writes, "In the final analysis, this book does no more than—from Jesus—raise the reality I have been experiencing into a theological concept, reflect on a christological faith I find as a living faith, and no more than present Christ, the great witness to God, from the sources in theology, of course, but also from the cloud of witnesses who shed light on the witness by definition."[5] By examining the reality around him, Sobrino shows us a new way to do theology. Seeing the downtrodden people around him, seeing the misery, the war, the poverty, the response is found in Jesus. The human Jesus, who suffered, was flogged, understands a people suffering. It is the divine Christ who resurrects and moves from the realm of the dead back to life. Reality is raised from the depths to the lofty realm of the conceptual. The downtrodden are raised from their crosses to triumph in Christ resurrected. The crucified Christ really is good news as a true liberator, Jesus Christ.

Sobrino insists that this image of the suffering Christ, also present in Spain and other Mediterranean cultures, uniquely becomes a symbol of protest in the South when it becomes a symbol of liberation. He associates this image of Jesus as liberator first and foremost with the historical Jesus of Nazareth. Following this historical Jesus necessitates a new way of living one's faith and this radical conversion can and does lead to the possibility of being murdered, especially for those who act in accordance with this novel image of Jesus the liberator. Martyrdom as a reality in Latin America proves that this new image for Christ is very real. The martyrs show evidence of a changed reality for those who want to fight for justice. By following Jesus more closely they put their own lives at risk.

The poor can be a locus for doing theology as well as a revelatory source. Ignacio Ellacuría also wrote of the poor as locus and finds in them evidence of both the kingdom of God as well as the anti-kingdom. The term that Sobrino attributes to Ellacuría to describe the oppressed majority is "the crucified people."[6] Sobrino's emphasis on the cross comes to the forefront, and he applies it to the most marginalized people in his society—the poor. Sobrino interprets God's revelation in his own reality to be read through the signs of the times, and finds this revelation in the people of God, the poor, the crucified people he sees around him.

Latin American Christology provides us with important tools for analyzing faith in Christ. Simply identifying with the image of Christ is not enough; one must act on one's faith in order for it to be faith. Sobrino writes, "Not only believers' 'image' of Christ, but their act of faith, their response to and correspondence in the reality of their lives with this image, helps christology to penetrate the reality of Christ and understand the texts about him."[7] The reason becomes clear why there must be a lived and active part of one's faith. The disciple and the martyr are two examples Sobrino uses for this lived faith. He writes, "Discipleship in practice is an introduction to the Jesus we follow, real martyrdom is an introduction to Jesus the martyr."[8] So do martyrs then necessarily come from the setting of the poor? In order to be a disciple of Christ does one have to walk in some way with the poor? Clearly for Sobrino discipleship involves some type of accompaniment or solidarity with the poor. But for now, I will leave the martyrdom question open, though it is also clear that El Salvador produced a number of martyrs who walked with the poor, like Rutilio Grande and the U.S. churchwomen, or spoke out against injustices against the poor, like Archbishop Romero. Nonetheless for Latin American Christology the important starting place is the situation of the poor. By walking with the poor a Christian better knows Christ.

THE KINGDOM, THE CROSS AND THE MARTYRS

Jesus's announcement of the kingdom of God is integrally connected to the poor. The essence of the Kingdom includes the life of the poor, and more than just defending their basic need to survive. There are two different time periods Sobrino addresses through this analysis. The first shows some of the historical background of Jesus and how Jesus addressed the poor in his day. But also he applies the strong Gospel images of Jesus to the problems the poor face in the world today. Archbishop Romero is one person who acts like Jesus and attempts to defend the lives of the poor. In the Gospels Jesus tries to convince others not just that God is good, but God has special compassion for the little ones, the *Anawim*, the poor. The good news brings with it a surprising crisis. While it is critical that everyone hear the good news, the people of Israel can no longer simply rely on their status as the chosen ones.

Finding the Kingdom leads to an expression of great joy and is a cause for celebration. Sobrino writes, "The coming of the Kingdom is good news, and is therefore incompatible with sadness. More, the Kingdom of God has to be celebrated with joy, since it would be a strange sort of good news if it did not."[9] While this Kingdom is celebrated against the backdrop of the anti-Kingdom, Jesus welcomes all of those people who most often are kept apart. For this reason Jesus invites the publicans, eats with sinners, and protects the prostitute. Even those not usually invited to the table can take part in the divine banquet. Jesus communicates the joy and happiness which the proclamation of the Kingdom causes to shine brightly forth both in his lifetime and today. The Kingdom can even cause us to celebrate now. And even though it may seem counter-intuitive to many, even the poor celebrate. Just because they may suffer more injustice than most does not mean that they are necessarily sad. Instead, "They have the capacity to celebrate what beneficent and liberative signs there are. And they celebrate it in community, like Jesus, around a table. This shared table is still the great sign of the Kingdom of God."[10] Rutilio Grande, SJ gave a famous homily at Apopa just a few weeks before he died. Rutilio preached about a common table for everyone, where each person had his or her own tablecloth and place setting. He named the table one of love, and ended the homily by proclaiming, "It is the love of shared fellowship that breaks and overthrows all types of barrier and prejudice and will overcome hate itself."[11]

It is impossible to overlook the deep identification with the cross in Latin America. Similar to the Spanish and Portuguese devotion, the popular identification with the cross cannot be underestimated. Holy Week in Bolivia, Chile, El Salvador and so forth, all have wide attendance at the procession behind the cross on Good Friday, and fewer people in attendance on Easter

Sunday.[12] Sometimes this may be due to a higher attendance at the Easter Vigil than can be found in the United States, but at its heart is the deep identification with a Christ who suffers for all sinners, but also a compassionate Jesus whose suffering many people in Latin America can identify with, in part because many are suffering themselves.

Latin American authors draw from this place of identification. Sobrino with the help of Ellacuría then moves it to the broader terminology of the crucified people. He writes,

> The crucified peoples of the Third World are today the great theological setting, the locus in which to understand the cross of Jesus. I say this because . . . a series of important questions appear which do not receive an unequivocal answer from exegesis: the meaning Jesus gave to his own death, the historicity of Jesus's trials, Jesus's last words on the cross, and so on . . . The point I do want to make is that the cross that dominates the Third World greatly illuminates the coherence with which the passion and death of Jesus—as a whole—are described.[13]

Since many people identify with the cross of Jesus it in turn helps them to carry their own cross. Sobrino then makes the locus of the crucified peoples his Christological starting point.

Sobrino recognizes that Jesus's teaching and preaching represented a radical threat to the established religious leaders of his time. The religious powers of the time, rather than deal with a radical message, simply snuffed it out. Jesus got in the way, and in the words of Romero, "Those that get in the way get killed."[14] But Jesus was persecuted by the authorities before his death on the cross. His active ministry, his healings, and his teaching caused a strong reaction by the establishment. The end result of the persecution is clear when Jesus enters the city of Jerusalem at the risk of loss of life for both him and his disciples. One need turn only to John's Gospel to learn that the death of Jesus is not accidental but the culmination of a historical process. Sobrino wants to show that this same persecution during the time of Jesus continues to occur with modern day disciples, most closely those who experience martyrdom. Thus, "It is important to stress in our time in order to grasp the element of culmination present in the murder of today's martyrs, and not to reduce them to a very cruel historical accident, but to understand them as something that could be seen coming, because history in itself is cruel."[15] Just as Jesus was persecuted, tortured and killed by death on a cross, so too are martyrs today being persecuted and killed.

The cross manifests the love of Jesus, and Jesus continues to fight for the poor despite the consequences. Sobrino claims, "The persecution arises because Jesus attacks the oppressors (historical dimension), who in addition justify oppression in the name of God (transcendent dimension). By attacking them, (Jesus) defends the victims."[16] Jesus consciously continues his course of actions to raise the plight of those on the margins to the consciousness of the mainstream. The increasing persecution does not slow Jesus's ministry. If anything his fervor increases. Jesus continued to fight for the poor despite the consequences. In the end, "This makes it clear that Jesus must have been aware of the possibility of a tragic outcome. This point is important to make us aware of Jesus's freedom and, ultimately, of his love."[17] Jesus stays in the fight despite knowing he might die. Sobrino sees the martyrs in a similar light. They don't shirk their responsibility nor run from persecution. Those who radically follow Jesus may end up dying like Jesus. Following Jesus as a disciple is fraught with conflict. But then again, so was Jesus's life. Jesus held to his convictions to his bitter end on the cross. As the cross joins with discipleship, if a person follows Jesus, for the love of Jesus's and Jesus's love for everyone, it may lead to conflict or even death.

Jesus did not die like some fanatical madman. He suffered persecution, willingly out of love, and in faithfulness to God. Sobrino adopts the thinking of the early Christian church in viewing Jesus as the first Christian martyr. If one understands the death of Jesus to be the first Christian martyr's death, perhaps it would be worth examining how Jesus viewed his own death. Similar to other prophetic figures, the historical Jesus may have tried to find meaning in his own death. The Eucharistic narratives in the Gospel may be one sign we have for Jesus's hope that his memory would live on. Especially in the narratives at the Last Supper, Jesus instituted something which would cause his memory to live on. Jesus links his own life and death to a life of service, a life lived for others. Jesus dies for all people in sacrificial service. Jesus's own sacrifice can thus be seen as an act of service, one which leads to the salvation of the human race. The first disciples are also invited to share in the sacrifice, especially in the cup of Jesus. Many may want this cup to pass by, as Jesus himself asked for in the agony of the garden. But the invitation to share in the cup is an invitation to share in the death of Jesus. A life of sacrifice and service may lead to drinking from this same cup, an invitation to all disciples even today. The prophet Micah serves as just one example. Jesus does justice, loves tenderly, and demands that we do the same. But this faithful service to the end is one which the martyrs take to heart.

Sobrino sees the death of Jesus as a consequence of his mission. The Gospels make it clear why he was killed, and in the world today there is nothing mysterious when many people die for political reasons as Jesus did. The tragedy lies in that so many human beings also suffer and die, but unlike the Son of God they go un-mourned, unremembered. Many martyrs for justice die uncelebrated, unremembered, unlike the proto-martyr Jesus who we remember in the Eucharist especially in the *anamnesis* prayer. Jesus dies because he gets in the way of the establishment, but he rises in the defense of the victims of this world. In the resurrection Jesus is recognized as the Son of God, the liberator.

VICTIMS AND VIOLENCE

The reality of the victims is vitally important, especially in Latin America. It is from this reality that martyrs are produced so this section addresses the violent situations which produce both victims and martyrs. As shown in the third and fourth chapters there is a long history of violence in Latin America, and especially in El Salvador, Sobrino's lived reality. For this reason the Latin American bishops's document from Medellín speaks out against such institutionalized violence, especially against forces of tyranny.[18] Archbishop Romero spoke out against this type of institutionalized violence, and died for it. He spoke out especially against institutionalized violence which perpetuates injustice, and wanted only those wars which satisfied traditional Catholic teaching regarding just war. Ignacio Ellacuría also analyzed this type of institutionalized violence and criticized it from different perspectives. First, structures which create violence must be examined against the common good. Second, "unjust violence" often perpetuates stereotypes and "generates the violence of repression."[19] Finally, Ellacuría makes the argument for revolutionary response against repression, if the repression works against the common good. The utilization of these terms were some of the reasons that politicians and military officials killed Ellacuría. They also made him an exemplary martyr for Sobrino, as one who died like Jesus, speaking out against the political regime and even religious authorities of his day.

Sobrino does not claim that violence is a solution proposed by Jesus but does believe that various kinds of violence need to be differentiated. Clearly Jesus suffered violence. And many in the Salvadoran civil war did too. The key question is how to explore a possible response to repressive violence. Structural violence and repressive injustice must be uncovered and confronted. In the end, all violence needs redemption and this redemption comes primarily from the person of Jesus Christ. The evil present in some societies needs to be redeemed. But some redemption also may come from the blood of the martyrs. Romero and Ellacuría remind us that the work and struggle for justice are not only important, but perhaps their deaths also brought an end to the violence. Their vocation was not one of armed insurrection. But they spoke out against the horrific violence they saw or heard about on a daily basis, and paid the ultimate price for it.

SCANDAL OF THE CROSS AND MARTYRDOM

The cross provides the link for explaining why Jesus died. First, one must acknowledge that it is not just any human person who dies on the cross but the Son of God. But Jesus was also killed like many of the prophets of God. He spoke out, or spoke differently from the powers that be, and was killed for it. Sobrino writes, "We may understand the historical reasons for the cross—Jesus's cross and those of so many others—but as to the 'why?' of the cross, judgment is suspended. If there is an explanation, it is hidden in God."[20] The death of Jesus forces us to answer the question of theodicy, not only why God allows evil in the world but also how is it that God can allow his only Son to die on the cross? The New Testament does not always provide convincing reasons. The passion plays commonly presented each year during Holy week do not necessarily reconcile the reasons behind why evil exists in the world. The cross expresses both hope and absurdity and goes beyond explanation. Sobrino criticizes those who would want to utilize only the Anselmian approach to explain the necessity of the cross. It may be one thing to appeal to God, "And it would be even more dangerous—as shown by all arguments based on Anselm—to claim to know that and how, in God, Jesus's cross becomes something logical and even necessary. If this were the case, Jesus cross would not reveal anything about God, it would not give any help at all in understanding God. God, understood in advance is what would make it possible to explain the cross, but then the cross would tell us nothing about God."[21] Moving beyond the scandal of the cross to the salvation of the cross is the mystery worth pondering.

There was a reason Jesus died a scandalous death on the cross. Formally speaking, there is goodness in the cross. God saved us from sin and God brings salvation through the cross. The crucified Jesus brings salvation from sin. But the type of sin is not specified by Jesus, whether personal or social, freedom from tyranny, or other type of sin. No strong distinctions are brought into question, rather those questions arise today. Second, God certainly saves through the person of Jesus. Sobrino writes, "But what specifically in the cross and what makes it a mediation of salvation, and in particular, forgiveness of sins, required explanation. Here, then we are moving on two levels: on the level of faith, the deeper level, where we affirm that there is salvation on the cross, and on the level of analysis, the more theological level, where we have to show how there can be salvation in the cross."[22] One could argue that especially on the theological level, the scandal of the cross should not be forgotten.

The martyrs serve as a reminder to those who might otherwise forget the scandal of the cross. One needs to accept the scandal of the cross along with the triumph of Jesus on the cross. Sobrino insists that "the pain of the cross does not in itself produce salvation."[23] Suffering by itself does not bring about redemption. But the cross demonstrates what was historically a necessary component of God's love. In many ways the whole of Jesus life led to the cross so that "real incarnation in a world of sin, is what leads to the cross, and the cross is the product of a real incarnation."[24] In this dichotomy incarnation to the cross, the cross moving to incarnation, encapsulates the whole of the life of Jesus. The incarnation of Jesus moves to the death of Jesus. But the fact that Jesus becomes flesh gives us the soteriological significance behind the cross.

This movement from incarnation to death and back again also reveals how one might view the martyrs. The martyrs lead us toward the mystery of the cross and serve as a reminder of the salvific dimension of the cross in a tangible way. The martyrs help faithful Christians in their own finitude here on earth, but also point toward the salvific nature of the cross. All people are born of a mother, and all of us will one day die. The martyrs help to remind Christians to follow the cross in discipleship. The cross can be understood through the example of one martyr especially, Archbishop Romero. Sobrino relates, "As often occurs in Latin America, in the presence of the martyrs, when human beings understand that there has been love, they understand it as good news, as something deeply humanizing. 'It is good for human beings that Archbishop Romero spent time on earth.'"[25] Romero serves as an example, someone who tried to pattern his life after Jesus in our day. While few people are called to martyrdom, the martyrs can inspire others by the depth of their sacrifice, and lead toward an ultimate identification with the saving love of the cross of Jesus.

MARTYRDOM AND THE CRUCIFIED PEOPLE

In *Jesus the Liberator* Sobrino links the cross to the "Crucified People."[26] With this methodological move Sobrino connects the scandalous death of Jesus on the cross with the suffering and death of many people in Latin America. Other Latin American authors have written about the suffering of many of the poor on the margins, but here the link becomes more tangible. When contemplating the scandal of the cross for Jesus, one might interpolate and better understand the suffering of so many. This contemplation does not encourage suffering for the sake of suffering; rather it examines the reality of suffering in the world. Sobrino reflects personally "What moves me to go deeply into the scandal of the cross is not that I am proposing a cult of suffering or masochism, or that I want to diminish the resurrection—some critics say I insist too much on what Paul says about the crucified Jesus and not enough on what he says about the risen Christ."[27] This reflection cautions that a person should not forget those who suffer like Christ did, and especially not forget the martyrs. The reality of the crucified people serves as a reminder of Jesus's own suffering on the cross. Personal experience also enters into an allusion to the UCA martyrs when Sobrino writes, "Allow me to say this with a very personal experience. On November 16, 1989, when the Jesuits of the Central American University were murdered outside their house, the body of Juan Ramón Moreno was dragged inside the residence into one of the rooms, mine. In the movement one book from the bookcase in the room fell on to the floor and became soaked in Juan Ramón's blood. The book was *The Crucified God*. It is a symbol, of course, but it expresses the themes of this chapter, God's real participation in the passion of the world."[28] This image is captured in a picture, and while only a symbol, it is eerily poignant. The book itself is conserved in the museum of the *Centro Monseñor Romero* at the UCA. This rare reflection on personal experience for Sobrino can also serve as a reminder that each of the exemplary martyrs in chapter 4 also had family and friends who remember their lives and the way they died. Learning about the UCA martyrs, Rutilio Grande, Romero, the U.S. churchwomen and others can deepen the reflection of every person, even if he or she does not have the same experience. Like Jesus these martyrs did not die a pleasant death.

Sobrino envisions Jesus's death as one of a trusting martyr. As Son of God, Jesus must have envisioned a meaningful death, but at the point of death he also must have placed all trust in God. But Jesus goes beyond the normal category of martyr. Sobrino writes, "Jesus on the cross is not presented as one more martyr, in the sense that the martyrs (or many of them) interpreted their own deaths in continuity with their lives and as their last service to their cause. They will disappear but their cause will go on, and their death will help the cause go on."[29] The death of Jesus goes beyond a fleeting cause, because on the cross, in spite of the apparent abandonment of Jesus by God the Father, Jesus completes his salvific mission.

Sobrino links the death of Jesus with the death of so many crucified people, those people who suffer because of poverty or injustice. In fact, the death of Jesus on the cross makes us remember "the crucified people." This term needs to be added as a part of a necessary theological language, since seeing the suffering of the crucified people helps us to identify the body of Christ in our midst. The crucified people, the poor, the marginalized, are the actual presence of the crucified Christ in history. Sobrino writes that "in this crucified people Christ acquires a body in history and that the crucified people embody Christ in history as crucified."[30] But the idea behind the crucified people can be further applied to the martyrs or "a martyred people."[31] As mentioned previously, Latin America is a place where recently more Christians have died a violent death than on any other continent. Many who are killed died as Jesus did, but are not called martyrs because they "do not fulfill the canonical and dogmatic conditions for martyrdom."[32] The current dogmatic requirements are similar to what was outlined in the first chapter: that martyrdom is caused by a death in *odium fidei* and death should not be a response to previous acts of violence, or revenge, on the martyr's part. In short, a martyr dies as a witness for the Christian faith.

Re-examining Jesus's death as a martyr sheds light on the Latin American context. For example, "The Latin American martyrs have forced us to rethink the traditional notion of martyrdom. In our opinion they have done something even more important: they have obliged theology to rethink its methodological approach to Christian martyrdom."[33] Christian martyrs in Latin America are in fact martyrs for the Kingdom of God. In this way "a martyr is defined as not only or principally someone who dies *for Christ*, but someone who dies *for Jesus's cause*. Martyrdom, in this definition, is not only death in fidelity to a demand of Christ's . . . but the faithful reproduction of Jesus's death. The essence of martyrdom is affinity with the death of Jesus."[34] The martyrs of Latin America cause us to rethink our definition, since many died for the same reasons Jesus did, in the attempt to bring about the Kingdom of God here on earth. But one might also add a new element to this definition, since a martyr can also be one who dies as a witness for justice. A martyr for justice can identify with Jesus on the cross in an ultimate way, "as the ultimate witness to God's love, particularly for victims and against their oppressors."[35] Sobrino stops short of calling those who died anonymously martyrs for the faith. I would agree and further declare that pushing the definition too far might dilute even an expanded definition. But whether they are called martyrs or not, it is clear that they often die an unjust death. While perhaps they do not show us the active struggle of the Kingdom, they are the ones who best illustrate the vast suffering poor of the world. What they do hold in common is an intense identification with the cross and a similarity to the martyrdom of Jesus.

Many martyrs structurally reproduce the martyrdom of Jesus, starting with Archbishop Romero, other exemplary martyrs as well as a myriad of priests, nuns, catechists, students, poor farm workers, and so forth. They died in a similar way to Jesus because they prophetically gave their lives for the Kingdom. But clearly Romero is a key martyr in El Salvador, now confirmed in his recent beatification. Romero stands out as one of the "martyred people" who gave his life for the cause of justice. This notion of a martyr for justice can be seen as a unique lens for interpreting Sobrino's Christology. Clearly Sobrino would assert that the death of Jesus on the cross reveals Jesus as the first martyr. In turn, reflection on the cross helps us to identify with "the crucified people." This identification reveals a new type of martyr which goes beyond the traditional definition, a martyr for the cause of justice.

THE JESUANIC MARTYR

Writing for the ten year anniversary of the UCA martyrs, Sobrino returns to the theme of martyrdom when he reflects on the deaths of his Jesuit companions.[36] In reflecting on the event, he coins a new term. In the article, he hearkens back to Rutilio Grande and Romero, Martin Luther King, and the proto-martyr Jesus of Nazareth, and advances the claim that the Salvadoran reality warrants the creation of a new category of martyr with a new name, "the Jesuanic martyr."[37] He links the term to Ellacuría's phrase, "the crucified people." The Jesuanic martyr can often be found in the same context which produces this crucified people and Sobrino affirms the nature of many in El Salvador who live as "a martyred people." The Jesuanic martyrs are authentic and with liberty and love denounce structural injustice and are not limited to El Salvador but are scattered throughout the global south.

These martyrs are characteristic of many Christians in Latin America who prophetically speak out against injustice on behalf of the poor. They are called Jesuanic martyrs because "their life, love and praxis are structurally like that of Jesus."[38] A Jesuanic martyr dies like Jesus and for the same cause as Jesus. This suggests a change to the traditional thinking on martyrdom. If once again I use Archbishop Oscar Romero as a primary example, it is because his life and death give us pause to account for not only an exceptional human being, but an excellent Christian example. For years many already proclaim him a saint because he spoke the truth and defended the poor from their oppressors. Romero's life is similar to that of Jesus Christ in life and death and he "reproduces the death of Jesus."[39]

There are two fundamental elements which all Jesuanic martyrs have in common: they act in "love and defense of their brothers, the poor, and they live out their lives, like Jesus, until death."[40] All of the Jesuanic martyrs, Romero, Martin Luther King, the UCA martyrs, respond to the anti-Kingdom by actively fighting for the Kingdom like Jesus did. The fight for the crucified people and their deaths express their love. So both the crucified people and the Jesuanic martyr must be linked together. Sobrino writes, "the crucified people is, definitely, what gives meaning to the Jesuanic martyr. They have been actively and freely incorporated with the death of the crucified people, and they have done it to save them, and have been saved by them."[41] The main difference between the martyrs of the UCA or other more famous martyrs is that unlike the crucified people their deaths are honored and remembered. But the deaths of these exemplary martyrs also remind us of the plight of the crucified peoples.

One of the main problems with the term Jesuanic martyr is that it falls outside the normal bounds of theological definition and category. Frankly put, until the papacy of Francis the church and theology simply have not known what to do with this new category of martyr.[42] Expanding the definition of martyrdom accounts for this new reality. The Jesuanic martyrs themselves call for this expansion with the way they give their lives in love. By the poignancy of their deaths, the UCA martyrs call all Christians to see the cross and the crucified people. They most profoundly identify with the mystery of God in the cross. They also call every Christian to conversion perhaps even towards death, "to give our lives to take the crucified people down from the cross."[43] To remember these Jesuanic martyrs is to remember all of the crucified people throughout the world. This remembrance of what the martyrs gave also reminds each person of the love of God and the call to be more fully human.

CHRIST THE LIBERATOR

The Jesuanic martyrs remind all Christians about the struggle for justice in this world. But in giving their lives to take the crucified people down from the cross, they also point us toward the resurrection. In *Christ the Liberator* Sobrino writes about the resurrection from the perspective of the victims of history. This book serves as a sequel to the previous book *Jesus the Liberator* and includes the impact of the resurrection, something which was purposely not included in the previous book. The work acknowledges the tremendous poverty in the world, and includes the perspective of the victims of history. Sobrino writes, "The view of the victims helps us to read christological texts and to know Jesus better. Furthermore, this Jesus Christ, known in this way, helps us to understand the victims better and, above all, to work to defend them."[44] The resurrection of Jesus also provides an important perspective on martyrdom since it can be seen as an eschatological event and one that irrupts into history. The resurrection can also bring hope to the hopeless, especially the poor and the marginalized throughout the world. The risen Christ claims victory over death on the cross. Martyrdom makes only a brief appearance in the first two of three sections in the book. I will reference these brief mentions of martyrdom and then shift to how Sobrino applies martyrdom in the third and final section of the book.

The third chapter outlines the hermeneutical principles necessary for understanding the resurrection from the perspective of the victims. The resurrection expresses the totality of being human and can be named as God's eschatological triumph over injustice. The resurrection of Jesus gives hope for all those crucified in history but also inspires Christian praxis. The hope in the resurrection should instill the desire to take the crucified people down from the cross. Sobrino asserts, "We can say that hope and action are needed to grasp Jesus's resurrection, and not just any love and action but those that apply to the task of taking the crucified down from the cross."[45]

Sobrino's first mention of martyrdom in the second part of the book occurs in chapter 12 in his discussion of the divine titles Son of God, Son of Man and Servant of Yahweh. In the discussion of these titles the problem of theodicy arises, especially because so many in Latin America suffer from inhuman poverty. In the face of injustice the only response is praxis, in contrast to those who choose to face the injustice with mere prayer or an inwardly directed faith. Just as the Son of God completed his mission here on earth, some people identify with the Son more fully and completely. Sobrino describes martyrdom in light of the divine title of Jesus as the Son of God: "In our world there are those who carry out a mission and are destroyed by it, ending up like the suffering servant, weak and powerless; there are many martyrs who today express this total identification with the servant."[46] The martyrs help to recall this suffering servant and raises awareness of those who are poor and die as victims. The suffering servant, Christ, is present to both the martyrs and the victims.

Martyrdom is also good news and the impact of Jesus's mercy can still be felt today. The martyrs help witness to the good news of Jesus and these keepers of the good news continue to inspire Christians to follow Jesus. Archbishop Romero and other Jesuanic martyrs witness to the good news through actions. For example, the good news converges in the person of Romero in three distinct ways. First, he brings the good news through his service to the Kingdom, his preaching, hope and utopia which he radiated. Second, Sobrino describes "his paschal fate, the ultimate solidarity and love his death expressed, and his hope of rising again in the Salvadoran people, whose liberation will come to be a reality."[47] Third, Romero evidenced solidarity with the poor by remaining close to the victims and prophetically speaking out against their oppressors. In short, Romero was good news to the poor and all those on the margins.

The death of Jesus and that of modern martyrs can be good news. There is a long litany of martyrs: Martin Luther King who speaks for the oppressed, Alfred Delp and Dietrich Bonhoeffer for speaking out against the Nazis, Ellacuría who returns to El Salvador despite the danger, and Ita, Maura, Jean, and Dorothy in their faithful accompaniment of the poor. Martyrdom is the epitome of good news and the good news brought by the martyrs almost always appears in times of persecution. Despite the faithful witness of Jesus as the proto-martyr the world today remains cruel. In spite of that cruelty, Sobrino recalls that "martyrs tell us that truth and love, firmness and faithfulness, and love to the end are possible. And that is good news."[48]

REALITY OF MARTYRDOM

The reality of martyrdom makes the strongest impact on the third part of *Christ the Liberator* which centers on Jesus Christ as mediator and the import of the Kingdom of God. The view of the victims, not only furthers the cause of liberation theology, but also shows how belief in Christ and working for the Kingdom takes into account the majority of the population of the world. Christology must be tied together with good works as the Christian community follows Christ as disciples in the post-Easter community. The apostles themselves show the importance of following Jesus and if tradition is correct virtually all of them died as martyrs. Whether or not this is legend one can insist on the eschatological significance of the witness of the twelve apostles as twelve martyrs. Sobrino argues, "Some of the great christologues, such as Ignatius of Antioch and Justin, died as martyrs and related, as we shall see, the reality of martyrdom to christology."[49] While none of the early church leaders formed a similar notion of the Jesuanic martyr, they did want to show how the reality they lived in produced martyrs who witnessed to their faith. The martyrs show us the need for witnessing to our faith so that faith not be relegated purely to the theoretical realm. The martyrs move us from complacent orthodoxy to active orthopraxy.

As Christianity moved to become a part of the mainstream Greco-Roman world, the martyrs still remained part of the Christian imagination. The Kingdom of God was still integrally tied to the gospel mission of service to the poor as well. But Sobrino argues that in some ways, the Christian imagination never lost a sense of the importance of standing against an oppressive regime or government. The first Christians understood the importance of what it meant to be a church of martyrs. Even as the church rose to a position of power, this tradition of martyrdom still remained.

These martyrs continually shape an understanding of how the victims of history view God and these victims still believe and hope in a powerful and saving God. But they also remain open to the notion of a God who suffers with them. The poor also have the ability to recognize those faith-committed people who choose to stand with them. Sobrino claims that in the experience of El Salvador many "have moved close to the victims—from Archbishop Romero and Ignacio Ellacuría to many other priests, religious sisters and professional people. Sociologically these people express otherness with regard to the poor, and it is just in this *otherness* that the victims see the possibility of salvation."[50] These exemplars of affinity with the poor choose to share the sufferings of the people even to the extent of experiencing martyrdom. Again Romero serves as an example of someone who witnesses to the church incarnate: "Romero saw something so saving in the cross, not just as the way to *resurrection* but as already the expression of incarnation and incarnation following on to the end; that is, he saw the cross as affinity—the greatest possible affinity—with victims."[51] Romero identified with the victims in the ultimate way, and for this reason the Salvadoran people believe he lives on with them, and continue to remember his witness at the anniversary of his death year after year.

The martyrs also help fight against the tendency of the church to gravitate toward docetism and gnosticism. They ground us in reality, and help the church to remember those who struggle daily for basic survival. Modern Christians remember Jesus as proto-martyr who as divine being also shared fully in our humanity through his death. One can never reject the possibility of martyrdom since doing so one also rejects salvation. For this reason Sobrino writes, "There is, therefore, a relationship between martyrdom and salvation, and the theoretical basis for this is communion in the (martyrial) flesh of both Jesus and the martyrs."[52] The martyrs show the Christian faithful the importance of witness, and the necessity for belief in something greater—salvation in Christ. The martyrs show the Docetists the importance of affirming both natures of Christ, human and divine, by following the life of Christ to the same ultimate end. One way to counter this Docetic impulse is to keep focusing on real life. It helps us to ground the church in a reality which accounts for those on the margins, rather than simply letting our ecclesial focus drift toward the sublime. Romero did not build a church without limitations, but he did build a real church. This real church served as a place for expressing grace, faith, commitment, and the hopes and values of the people of El Salvador. This same church stood with the poor and the victims evidenced by the priests, women religious, and committed church members who gave their lives in witness and in solidarity with the poor.

When trying to find God in history martyrdom again sheds light on the cross as sacrifice or self-giving. The cross becomes a symbolic part of history and emphasizes how Jesus came into conflict with the oppressors. Sobrino claims, "The cross came about, therefore, for defending the weak, and this makes it an expression of love. We can then say that the cross brings salvation, that the cross is *eu-aggelion*, good news. Love saves, and in the end love, in its various expressions, is the only thing that saves."[53] Jesus's love culminates in the cross, a radical expression of self-giving throughout his life. Some want to qualify this love, just as some debate how to qualify Romero's love in his canonization process. Many debate what title to give Romero if he is to be canonized. Sobrino writes, "If he is to be beatified as a martyr (and not as bishop and martyr), what counts essentially from the canonical point of view is his death itself, which could mean that his past life and the historical reasons that led to his death—with the exceptions of the hatred of the faith and now, perhaps the hatred of justice—will not be essential, or at best be secondary."[54] But in many ways this would distort the real person in history. To omit the justice issues, the fact that he defended the poor against his oppressors and died in the end for it, would distort the reasons for his martyrdom in history. The martyrs remind the church of the Jesus of history as well. The resurrection of Jesus is that much more powerful after he lived in the Galilee, healed the sick, broke bread with his disciples and then died a scandalous death on the cross. For this reason, Sobrino claims that the resurrection as a part of history is greater than a resurrection which is purely conceptual. The risen Christ did in fact walk among us. The resurrection "is doing justice to a victim; it is the hope that the butcher will not triumph over the victims and that we may be able to share in this hope."[55] The cross and the resurrection joined together as one unity reveal the God of love.

Christ the Liberator ends with an excursus on journey and memory. This conclusion demonstrates the centrality of the Kingdom of God and the important status of the poor in the Kingdom. The Kingdom of God calls the disciples of Jesus to faithfulness, to walk humbly and follow the call of Jesus Christ. The Christian message should also give hope to the victims. Martyrs provide an example of those who follow Jesus to the ultimate end. They are the witnesses and give the poor and the victims reason for hope. Sobrino names these witnesses when he recalls, "Archbishop Romero, Ignacio Ellacuría and his companions, Celina Ramos, and most recently Juan Gerardi—a whole constellation of witnesses, martyrs who not only bear witness to Christ but who remake the life and fate of Jesus."[56] These martyrs bring hope and can be the mediation of grace for the crucified peoples, the victims of this world. These victims also stubbornly show us how to hope against hope. The victims help us to remember what is important, but also what it means to journey clinging to hope. The martyrs encourage us to live our faith more authentically with the witness of their lives. Sobrino closes poignantly, "But the greatest encouragement comes from those who inspire with their actual lives, those who today resemble Jesus by living and dying as he did. This is God's journey to this world of victims and martyrs, and is the way to the Father and the way to human beings, above all to the poor and the victims of this world."[57]

The importance of an expansion of the definition of martyrdom has required some new terminology. The crucified people, the martyred people, martyrs for justice, and the Jesuanic martyr all help provide fuel for this expansion. But some think theologians may try to expand the definition too far. What if canonizing Romero serves as a flood gate for the naming of martyrs? If we name more anonymous martyrs might this in the end drain the term of all meaning? For this reason it is important to have a solid definition of a martyr in the twenty-first century and shows how the naming of more martyrs can help remind us of the victims of history, those on the margins, and those many disappeared and even nameless martyrs who might otherwise be forgotten.

NOTES

1. These are the full titles of both books but from here forward I will reference the two books as Jesus the Liberator and Christ the Liberator taken from the English book titles from Orbis Books. The original Spanish titles are actually a bit more specific: *Jesucristo Liberador. Lectura historica-teológica de Jesús de Nazaret* published two years before the English version in 1991 and *La Fe en Jesucristo: Ensayo desde las víctimas* published in 1999.

2. Sobrino, Jon. *Jesus the Liberator: A Historical-Theological View*. Translated by Paul Burns and Francis McDonagh. Maryknoll, NY: Orbis Books, 1993, 5.

3. *Jesus the Liberator*, 8.

4. Ibid.

5. Ibid.

6. *Jesus the Liberator*, 26. This phrase "the crucified people" originally appeared in an article by Ignacio Ellacuría "Discernir el 'signo' de los tiempos," Diakonía 17 (1981), p. 58.

7. *Jesus the Liberator*, 27.

8. Ibid, 28.

9. Ibid, 102.

10. Ibid, 104.

11. Ibid, 104. The homily can be found in its entirety in the *Revista ECA* 348/347 (1977) p. 859.

12. While I admit I have no "hard data" on this, it is fairly obvious to one who has lived in these countries the vast numbers who participate in the Good Friday processions and devotions versus the attendance at the Easter Sunday masses when people "dress their Sunday best."

13. Ibid, 196.

14. Ibid.

15. Ibid, 199.

16. Ibid, 200. I insert the word Jesus for sake of clarity.

17. Ibid.

18. See especially the sections on "Peace" from Medellín, numbers 16 and 19.
19. *Jesus the Liberator*, 213. Sobrino does not cite the explicit document here, but may be paraphrasing here from one of Ellacuria's articles, "Violence and non-Violence."
20. Ibid, 221.
21. Ibid.
22. Ibid, 222. Sobrino cites numerous biblical citations in this section to prove the idea of a primitive kerygma, Acts 5:31, John 11:50, Cor 5:14 ff, for example.
23. Ibid, 228.
24. Ibid, 229.
25. Ibid, 230. The quote inside the quote is from Ellacuría.
26. Ibid, 233. As mentioned previously the idea of "the crucified people" is borrowed in part from Ignacio Ellacuría. What is novel here is the methodological move to link the cross to the crucified peoples which Sobrino adopts from Ellacuría. See Ignacio Ellacuría's article in *Mysterium Liberationis*, "The Crucified People" p. 580–603.
27. Ibid, 235. One needs to remember as well that Sobrino will deal more with the risen Christ in his next book *Christ the Liberator*.
28. Ibid, 235.
29. Ibid, 238.
30. Ibid, 255.
31. Ibid, 265.
32. Ibid.
33. Ibid, 266.
34. Ibid, 267. Italics author's emphasis.
35. Ibid, 269.
36. Sobrino, Jon. "Los Mártires Jesuánicos Y El Pueblo Crucificado." *Paginas* XXV, no. 161: 45–61. The article was originally published in a small Salvadoran journal *Vida Nueva* in 1999.
37. Ibid, 45.
38. Ibid, 47.
39. Ibid. "Reproduce la muerte de Jesús." On this page Sobrino also mentions Pedro Casaldáliga's poem "San Romero de América" to further the case for sainthood.
40. Ibid, 48. "El amor y la defensa a los hermanos, los pobres, y al llevarlo a cabo, como Jesús, hasta la muerte."
41. Ibid, 50. "Pues bien, el pueblo crucificado es, en definitiva, lo que da sentido a los mártires jesuánicos. Estos se han incorporado activa y libremente a la muerte del pueblo crucificado, lo han hecho para salvarlo, y han sido salvados por él."
42. While John Paul II made an attempt with the idea of a martyr for charity, it is Francis who has asked for an expanded definition.
43. Ibid, 51. I add crucified people for meaning. "Hasta dar nuestras vidas, por bajarlos de la cruz."
44. Sobrino, Jon. *Christ the Liberator: A View from the Victims*. Translated by Paul Burns. Maryknoll, NY: Orbis Books, 2001, 8.
45. Ibid, 49.

46. Ibid, 189.
47. Ibid, 216.
48. Ibid, 217.
49. Ibid, 229.
50. Ibid, 272. Italics author's emphasis.
51. Ibid, 273. Italics author's emphasis.
52. Ibid, 279.
53. Ibid, 305.
54. Ibid, 306.
55. Ibid.
56. Ibid, 340.
57. Ibid.

Conclusion

The Reality of Martyrdom Today

A new definition of martyrdom for the twenty-first century is necessary in response to the call of Pope Francis. Pope Francis, before the announcement of the beatification of Oscar Romero, first asked theologians to propose an expanded definition which might take into account Romero and other martyrs who gave their lives in purportedly Roman Catholic countries. It will be helpful to first examine recent scholarship of Sobrino on the Salvadoran martyrs. Second, since we now have an ecclesial document for Romero's beatification we can discuss its criteria for martyrdom. Third, a three-tiered ideal for martyrdom is proposed, which derives in part from applying the insights of the second Vatican Council to the situation here in the United States. Fourth, it is possible to challenge Sobrino's ideas concerning the anonymous martyr and the problems with extending the term too far. Finally, the importance of remembrance must be developed in order to demonstrate the importance of a reformulated description of the meaning of martyrdom in the contemporary Catholic Church.

THE CALL OF POPE FRANCIS AND SOBRINO'S RECENT REFLECTIONS ON MARTYRDOM

In 2014 when asked about the potential beatification of Oscar Romero, Pope Francis intimated that the current definition of martyrdom is insufficient to account for all martyrs in the twentieth and twenty-first centuries.[1] While the traditional definition has served the Church well for centuries, the modern era has introduced a new problematic. The definition, to die for the faith in *odium fidei*, still serves its intended function when a Christian is killed by a non-Christian, but in this post-modern and pluralistic world, what happens when a Christian is killed by a fellow Christian for values which stem from the martyr's faith? This section explores this new problematic. But rather than argue that this is merely a readjustment or an expansion of a more traditional definition, it can be argued that lived reality in the twentieth and twenty-first centuries calls for a new interpretation of martyrdom. In the end, the reasons for blocking certain Christians from being officially declared martyrs has more to do with politics or a rigid ecclesiological framework than it does with the life, testimony and witness of the person under consideration for the title martyr. It is certainly true that in the case of Archbishop Romero, if he had been declared a martyr after his death, he could immediately have been declared a saint.[2]

In some ways Sobrino's thinking on martyrdom has changed very little since his writings in 2003, and his various reflections after the death of the Jesuits and lay women companions in 1989. But at times one can discern a polemical tendency in Sobrino which is likely a bi-product of some of the investigations into his Christology. In many ways these investigations appeared to be something of a retaliation against his sharp critique of outdated church structures and church leadership in El Salvador. It is not necessary to mention all of the details of these investigations here. But rightly or wrongly, Sobrino has in recent years responded with some sharp public statements regarding the deaths of Rutilio Grande, Romero and his brother Jesuits. As mentioned previously the photos of Grande, Romero, and Ellacuría face his desk at the UCA and serve as a constant reminder of their witness.

Around the time of the thirty-fifth anniversary of the death of Romero some people spoke as if it did not really matter if they declared Romero a martyr or a saint. I found this idea surprising and was perplexed about its meaning. I saw first-hand at the 25th anniversary of the death of the Jesuits at the UCA and their two laywomen collaborators in 2014 at the mass in Romero's tomb, how much people revere him. Throughout the mass people walked over to the tomb, knelt and prayed, or even kissed the tomb or laid flowers there. Popularly Romero is already revered as a martyr and a saint. Therefore, whether or not Romero is canonized many people have already popularly declared him a martyr and a saint. But I would argue that declaring Romero a martyr and a saint does in fact matter. It matters to many people in El Salvador, and would constitute a validation, and for some the rectification of an injustice that it has taken so long to beatify him (not to mention the wait for his actual canonization). But as discussed in the argument of the anonymous martyr at the end of this chapter, sometimes Sobrino appears to have pushed his idea of what constitutes a martyr too far.

One consistency over time for Sobrino has been his adherence to the idea of a Jesuanic martyr, one who dies like Jesus. More recently he has also advanced the idea of a martyr for justice, and the importance of the martyrs lies in the fact that they remind us of those who die more anonymously. Perhaps the Vatican II ideal of saints with a capital "S" and a small s might be relevant here. One can identify at least three types of martyrs in general. First there are the official martyrs declared by the church and the exemplary martyrs in modern times which are in the process of being accounted for. These are the exemplary martyrs detailed in chapter 4, but also many other Martyrs with a capital "M" who can be found throughout Latin America. These Martyrs then remind us of so many anonymous martyrs, martyrs with a small m, those lay catechists, brothers, sisters, who died while living out their faith. And finally remembering these capital "M" Martyrs and small m martyrs, allows us to think about the more anonymous or unknown martyrs. There may be more anonymous martyrs who remain unknown to us entirely, in a similar way to Rahner's idea of the anonymous Christian, those who live Christian lives without ever having heard about Jesus Christ. But we might not want to push this last idea of martyrdom too far, since it might dilute the meaning of the term. The Martyrs do help the church account for those who were slaughtered, professing their faith, living values of faith and justice and were "disappeared" or tortured and then killed, sometimes their broken bodies lying in an unknown mass grave. It might be tenuous to call them martyrs even in an expanded sense, but there is no doubt that remembering how the exemplary martyrs like the U.S. churchwomen died, can also lead to an accounting of who they were fighting for, advocating for, ministering to, and for whom they were willing to die for prematurely. And here, to borrow a thought from Sobrino, it does not matter if they are ever officially categorized as martyrs, these anonymous ones, as long as they are in fact counted as giving their Christian lives in faith to the bitter end. But it is important that the exemplary martyrs find a place in the church of today with a theologically adequate definition.

In a short talk delivered in Madrid in 1992, Sobrino outlines the important link between the cross of Jesus and martyrdom. Martyrs today continue to help us remember why Jesus died. Particularly in the global north it is an important reminder, they killed Romero for the same reasons they killed Jesus, to silence the truth. For this reason, "Today's martyrs are martyrs *in* the church, but not *of* the church. They are martyrs *of* humanity, *of* the poor."[3] The martyrs not only serve as a reminder of the cross but also of the plight of the poor. For this reason these martyrs have shown great love as Jesus did, and an expanded definition is necessary to more deeply remember them as saints for their witness. They also help one to remember "the anonymous and passive martyrs: children, the elderly women, those who are killed simply for being poor and to keep them from trying to be anything else. Killed in their total defenselessness, without weapons of war . . . in their total innocence . . . often lacking even the opportunity to escape death."[4] Remembering the exemplary Martyrs[5] then also allows the church to account for those poor who may be forgotten (anonymous martyrs), and through remembering them restore credibility to faith.

Martyrs also need to be better accounted for in the global south, but especially in Latin America. Here Sobrino's idea behind the Jesuanic martyrs is a helpful one. The Martyrs practice their faith as Jesus did and were killed for it. In other words, "the necessary material condition for martyrdom is a violent death, but the formal condition is that such a death must be, in some way an *expression* and (without falling into sterile casuistry) the *culmination* of a praxis of defending and loving the poor and oppressed, as Jesus's death was."[6] This shifts the definition from a more classic definition *in odium fidei* toward a more active definition for one who dies like Jesus or for the cause of Jesus. This can also be equated to being martyred for hatred of truth and justice, and not simply hatred of one's Christian faith. This movement to have these modern martyrs accounted for goes beyond mere symbolism. Instead it allows for an accounting of the signs of the times as outlined in *Gaudium et Spes*, 4. As Sobrino correctly demonstrates, "The Latin American martyrs . . . shine a light on the truth of our world and express love for the poor of this world. In this way they 'verify' the truth that there is salvation in the cross of Jesus."[7] The Martyrs not only remind Christians of the plight of the poor, but also point the way to salvation through the death and resurrection of Jesus Christ.

The Martyrs then provide us with both a prophetic challenge and a reconciling grace. They wake us from our dogmatic slumber but also call us to greater solidarity with the worldwide church and the plight of the marginalized. As Pope Francis recently suggested in *Laudato Si'* the globalized world sometimes leaves out those with the greatest economic challenges. Sobrino reminds us of Romero's ideal of a real church still applies today:

> a church cannot be real that is not poor in times of poverty, not persecuted in times of persecution . . . that is not hopeful in times of hope, and does not encourage hope in times of discouragement. "To overcome unreality," it seems to us, is the martyrs first challenge to the church today. But they are also a grace for the Church. Their example and their memory are an inspiration for the task.[8]

The Martyrs call the church to assume the burden of reality to continue to work for the salvation of all people not just those with money, power and influence. Rutilio Grande preached about the Cains and Abels of society and the fact that there continue to be some in the world who reap the benefits of permitting people at the margins to die premature and unjust deaths. One can understand that this is not just a literal slaughtering of people but a slow and painful death through back-breaking work, poor access to food, water, shelter, adequate health care, and so forth. This is the cross which Sobrino alludes to and which the martyrs challenge the rest of the church to assume. This challenge acts as a necessary correction to an overtly pious response, to simply pray for the less fortunate, rather than hearing a call to action to right systemic injustices. Assuming this reality then allows the church to continue to believe in martyrs today. As Sobrino claims, "The Latin American Church has been a persecuted and martyrial church. Objectively, its martyrs are like Jesus because they followed Jesus to the end, and were killed as a direct result of defending the oppressed, as Jesus was—thus, as witness to the God of life. They are martyrs of the kingdom of God and of humanity."[9]

THE IMPORTANCE OF THE BEATIFICATION OF OSCAR ROMERO

The beatification of Oscar Romero opens the door for an expansion of the definition of martyrdom. Recently it became possible to examine the official document outlining Romero's cause for sainthood.[10] Throughout the text Romero is referred to as a Martyr. But surprisingly, the text does little to advance the theological work called for by Pope Francis. While a criterion can be inferred, no place in the document does it articulate a reason why Romero should be considered a Martyr. It is often simply presumed. In some ways this is to be expected. The work is an official ecclesial document, and one that attempts to document the rationale behind the case for Romero's canonization. But clearly if and when Romero is canonized it will be as a Martyr and a Saint. The text does infer that Romero was killed for values which stem from his faith, as Rahner alludes to, and also that he lived a virtuous life and fought for truth and justice. But the justice theme stops short of calling Romero a martyr for justice or a Jesuanic martyr as Sobrino does. Perhaps for political or ecclesiological reasons the document at times makes more reference to his humble and austere life, that he was a faithful bishop, and obedient to Rome, than of his much lauded work for human rights, preaching to bring to light the abuses which the poor suffered including disappearances and torture, and his role as shepherd in a church which found itself under siege from right wing government and para-military forces. While the document does allow one to better understand the person of Romero, especially in terms of his biographical history, it is a significantly different account than those offered by native Salvadorans. While this account of Romero may have been necessary to ease the process of becoming a saint, it does little to offer theologians with significantly new criteria for an expanded definition of martyrdom today.

THREE TIERED EXPANSION OF MARTYRDOM

Between Cunningham, Rahner, Sobrino and others there is enough material to propose an expanded definition of martyrdom for today. The traditional definition still holds true; a martyr can still be a witness to the faith who is killed in *odium fidei*. But Rahner's challenge to martyrdom with its threefold categories should also be considered. The third criterion carries a special weight. A man or woman should be considered a martyr if they die for the values which stem from their faith. Sobrino's terminology is also helpful. The Latin American reality brings a new type of martyr, a martyr who dies like Jesus—a Jesuanic martyr, and a martyr for justice. There are some atrocities and human rights abuses which are worth crying out to the heavens about, even if it means dying as a voice for justice. Rutilio Grande, Romero, the U.S. churchwomen, and Ellacuría and his brother Jesuits at the UCA all can be named martyrs on this basis. One can also add to this list based on the different Latin American countries, Archbishop Girardi in Guatemala, Sister Dorothy Stang in Brazil, and other examples more recent than 1989. All of these martyrs died for the hatred of the faith, the martyrs for justice, and these exemplary martyrs are all Martyrs with a capital "M." These exemplary martyrs allow the church to remember those more anonymous martyrs. In some of the CEBs in El Salvador for example they commemorate at a celebration each year all of those lay catechists, those men, women and children of faith who died speaking out against torture and the disappeared. For me, these are martyrs with a small "m." Clearly they are martyrs who died because of values which stem from their faith, but due to their social status or lack of publicity they are remembered only locally. Throughout Latin America there are many people who would fall into this category.

There are at least two types of anonymous martyrs which also demand attention. First they are those martyrs who were practicing Christians but it is less obvious that they died from values stemming from their faith. Two cases from chapter 2 fall into this category. First, the two lay women who died alongside of the Jesuits at the UCA. While popularly they have been considered martyrs alongside the Jesuits, the reason they stayed at the UCA that night was for safety concerns in traveling home, not in a stance of justice or solidarity. Their case for martyrdom is thus less clear. Similarly, while they were Christians, those killed in the massacre at El Mozote were likely killed for being in the wrong place at the wrong time. The military attacked them for purportedly harboring rebel forces, later proved untrue, but not because they were decrying faith and justice issues in San Salvador. In fact, the majority in that Christian community had chosen not to support either side in the war. Other cases which Sobrino proposes at different points in his writing were the "red martyrs," communist students marching for justice during the Salvadoran civil war, as well as non-Christians who fight for justice such as Gandhi. I would suggest that here Sobrino's polemic side may take him too far. While there may be a case for Elba and Celina Ramos and those Christians killed at El Mozote to one day be declared martyrs, I think it is a slippery slope opening the formal question of martyrdom to those who are non-believers. There must be some element of Christian faith present or this proposal for an expanded definition will expand so far as to become superfluous. For this expanded definition to carry weight, the element of Christian faith in addition to being killed for the fight for truth and justice or values stemming from that faith must also be present.

REMEMBERING THE MARTYRS

It is my sincere hope that in proposing this expanded definition of martyrdom we do not lose sight of the issues surrounding the deaths of these martyrs. During the celebration of the twenty fifth anniversary year of the deaths of the Martyrs of the UCA, Kevin Burke, SJ gave an outstanding lecture at Marquette University extolling the value of remembering the martyrs.[11] Remembering the Martyrs takes us back to the early origins of the church, a time when the saints and martyrs were held with great reverence. But the Martyrs of today also remind us of the dangerous memory of Jesus which Johann Baptist Metz details so eloquently. These Martyrs who die like Jesus, speaking out for truth and justice through words and deeds must be remembered. Remembering them allows for those more local martyrs to also be remembered. By remembering them the church can also remember those who died or were killed as anonymous martyrs. Finally, when the church remembers its Martyrs it also remembers not only the great witness to the faith, but the plight of the poor, those on the margins, and those who struggle for more justice and equality in the world. Grande, Romero, the U.S. churchwomen, the Martyrs of the UCA all call us to remember that sometimes the world is not only unfair but unjust, and that Jesus continues to challenge all Christians to build the kingdom of God on earth each and every day. The most recent Latin American Bishops Conference at Aparecida calls all Christians to become missionary disciples of Jesus. It articulates that this call is sometimes radically prophetic and capable of showing the light of Christ to the world. Furthermore those who preach this radically prophetic message "continue the tradition of so many consecrated men and women saints and martyrs in the long history of the Continent."[12] These witnesses call all Christians to greater faith and the promotion of justice. By remembering these modern Martyrs, the church renews its commitment to the poor, to those on the margins, and to the salvation of all Christian souls.

NOTES

1. In an August 19, 2014, Zenit.org published Interview, Pope Francis hinted at expanding the theological category of martyrdom beyond *odium fidei*, and mentioned Archbishop Romero and Rutilio Grande specifically.

2. One could argue that the political atmosphere, and the infighting between ecclesiological camps in El Salvador had more to do with the delay in considering Romero's canonization, than the way he lived his life, his witness or his call to holiness, for example.

3. Sobrino, Jon. *Witnesses to the Kingdom: The Martyrs of El Salvador and the Crucified Peoples*. New York: Orbis Books, 2003, 109. Italics author's emphasis.

4. *Witnesses to the Kingdom*, 109.

5. I am purposefully capitalizing the word Martyr each time I use it when I refer to these exemplary martyrs, martyrs for justice, paradigmatic martyrs, and so forth.

6. Ibid, 122. Italics author's emphasis.

7. Ibid, 128.

8. Ibid, 142.

9. Ibid, 154.

10. Due to the copyright issues I am only paraphrasing from the text. The large red tome is titled *Beatificationis Seu Declarationis Martyrii Servi Dei Ansgarii Arnolfi Romero*, Positio Super Martyrio, Roma, Tipografia Nova Res s.r.l, Piazza di Porta Maggiore, 2, 2014.

11. Marquette University Symposium on the Martyrs of the UCA, October, 2014.

12. Aparecida, #220. Full quote in Spanish, "Esta llamada a ser una vida misionera, apasionada por el anuncio de Jesús-verdad del Padre, por lo mismo, radicalmente profética, capaz de mostra a la luz de Cristo las sombras del mundo actual y los senderos de vida nueva, para lo que se requiere un profetismo que aspire hasta la entrega de vida, en continuidad con la tradición de santidad y martirio de tantas y tantos consagrados a lo largo de la historia del Continente."

Bibliography

Ashley, J. Matthew. "Apocalypticism in Political and Liberation Theology." *Horizons* 27, no. 1 (2000): 22–43.
———. "Forjando Una Espiritualidad Ecclesial, La Espiritualidad Y La Reliogisidad De Monsenor Oscar A. Romero." *Revista Latinoamericana de Teologia* 64, no. 22 (2005): 27–44.
Bergman, Susan. *Martyrs*. New York: Harper Collins 1996.
Berrios, Fernando, Costadoat, SJ, Jorge, Garcia, Diego ed. *Signos De Estos Tiempos: Interpretacion Teologica De Nuestra Epoca*. Santiago, Chile: Ediciones Universidad Alberto Hurtado, 2008.
Berryman, Phillip. *Stubborn Hope: Religion, Politics and Revolution in Central America*. Maryknoll, New York: Orbis Books, 1994.
Bombonatto, Vera Ivanise. *Seguimento De Jesus: Uma Abordagem Segundo a Cristologia De Jon Sobrino*. Sao Paulo, Brazil: Paulinas, 2002.
Brockman, James R. SJ. *Romero: A Life*. Maryknoll, New York: Orbis Books, 1989.
———. ed. *Oscar Romero: The Violence of Love*. Farmington, PA: The Plough Publishing House, 1998.
———. *La Violencia Del Amor: Mons. Oscar A. Romero*. Bilbao, Spain: Editorial Sal Terrae, 2002.
Budi, Hartono. "The Christology of Jon Sobrino and Contemporary Martyrdom." Dissertation, Graduate Theological Union, 1999.
Burke, Kevin. "Book Review: Christ the Liberator." *Theological Studies* 63, no. 4 (2002): 859–61.
Camara, Dom Helder. *Dom Helder Camara: Essential Writings*. Maryknoll, New York: Orbis Books, 2009.
Campbell-Johnston, Michael. S.J. "Monsenor Romero: Westminster a Roma." *Cuadernos Monsenor Romero*, (1998).
Cardenal, Rodolfo. *Historia De Una Esperanza: Vida De Rutilio Grande*. San Salvador, El Salvador: UCA Editores, 1985.

Carranza, Salvador. *Rutilio Grande: Martir De La Evangelizacion Rural En El Salvador*. San Salvador, El Salvador: UCA Editores, 1978.

———. *Romero-Rutilio: Vidas Encontradas*. San Salvador, El Salvador: UCA Editores, 1992.

———. *Una Luz Grande Nos Brillo: Rutilio Grande, S.J.* San Salvador, El Salvador: UCA Editores, 1997.

Carrigan, Ana. *Salvador Witness: The Life and Calling of Jean Donovan*. New York: Simon and Schuster, 1984.

———. *Salvador Witness: The Life and Calling of Jean Donovan*. Revised ed. Maryknoll, NY: Orbis Books, 1984, 2005.

Casaroli, Agostino. *The Martyrdom of Patience: The Holy See and the Communist Countries (1963–1989)*. Translated by Fr. Marco Bagnarol. Toronto, Canada: Ave Maria Centre of Peace, 2007.

Casas, Bartolome de Las. *The Only Way to Evangelize*. Translated by S.J. Francis Patrick Sullivan, Edited by Helen Rand Parrish. New York: Paulist Press, 1992.

Cavada, Miguel. *Monsenor Romero: Su Vida, Su Testimonio Y Su Palabra*. San Salvador, El Salvador: Equipo Maiz, 1999.

———. ed. *Homilias: Monsenor Oscar A. Romero*. Vol. 1. San Salvador, El Salvador: UCA Editores, 2005.

———. ed. *Homilias: Monsenor Oscar A. Romero*. Vol. 6. San Salvador, El Salvador: UCA Editores, 2009.

Chandler, Andrew, ed. *The Terrible Alternative: Christian Martyrdom in the 20th Century*. London: Cassell, 1998.

Cunningham, Lawrence. *The Meaning of Saints*. San Francisco: Harper and Row, 1980.

———. "Saints and Martyrs: Some Contemporary Considerations." *Theological Studies* 60, (1999): 529–537.

———. "On Contemporary Martyrs." *Theological Studies* 63, (2002): 374–81.

———. *A Brief History of Saints*. Malden, MA: Blackwell Publishing, 2005.

———. "Causa Non Poena: On the Contemporary Martyrs." In *More Than a Memory: The Discourse of Martyrdom and the Construction of Christian Identity in the History of Christianity*, edited by Johan Leemans, 451–64. Dudley, MA: Peeters, 2005.

Cynthia Glavac, O.S.U. *In the Fullness of Life: A Biography of Dorothy Kazel, O.S.U.* Denville, NJ: Dimension Books, 1996.

Delgado, Jesus. *Oscar A. Romero: Biografia*. 2nd ed. San Salvador, El Salvador: UCA Editores, 1994.

Dennis, Golden and Wright, ed. *Oscar Romero: Reflections on His Life and Writings*. New York: Orbis Books, 2000.

Diaz, Carlos. *Monsenor Oscar Romero*. Vol. 4. Salamanca: Colleccion Sinergia, KADMOS, 2003.

Diaz, Miguel. "La Autoridad En La Iglesia. Palabra Y Testimonio De Monsenor Romero." *Revista Latinoamericana de Teologia* 40, no. 14 (1997): 3–16.

Diaz, Ruben Murillo, ed. *Noviembre De 1989: El Asesinato De Los Jesuitas En El Salvador*. Mexico City: Universidad Iberoamericana, 1990.

Diez, Miguel Cavada, ed. *Homilias: Monsenor Oscar A. Romero*. Edited by UCA Editores. Vol. 1. San Salvador, El Salvador: UCA Editores, 2005.
Doggett, Martha. *Death Foretold: The Jesuit Murders in El Salvador*. Washington D.C. : Georgetown University Press, 1993.
Eagleson, Torres and, ed. *The Challenge of Basic Christian Communities*. New York: Orbis Books, 1982.
Ellacuria, Ignacio. "M. Romero Un Enviado De Dios Para Salvar a Su Pueblo." *Revista Latinoamericana de Teologia* 19, no. 7 (1990): 5–10.
———. "Aporte De La Teologia De La Liberacion." In *Escritos Teologicos*. San Salvador, El Salvador: UCA Editores, 2002.
———. *Escritos Teologicos*. San Salvador, El Salvador: UCA Editores, 2002.
———. "Tesis Sobre La Posibilidad De La Teologia Latinoamerica." In *Escritos Teologicos*. San Salvador, El Salvador: UCA Editores, 2002.
Erdozain, Placido. *Archbishop Romero: Martyr of El Salvador*. Maryknoll, NY: Orbis Books, 1984.
Fiorenza, Francis. "Book Review: Christ the Liberator." *Theology Today* 59, no. 2 (2002): 326–30.
Garcia, Maria Candelaria. *Un Legado De Amor*. 2nd ed. San Salvador: Impresas Quijanos, 2005.
Gonzalez Faus, Jose Ignacio. "Las Victimas Como Lugar Teologico." *Revista Latinoamericana de Teologia*, no. No. 46 (1999): 89–104.
Grande, Rutilio "Violencia Y Situacion Social." *ECA* 262, (1970): 369–75.
Guerra, Walter, ed. *Testigos De La Fe En El Salvador: Nuestros Sacerdotes Y Seminaristas Diocesanos Martires 1977–1993*. San Salvador, El Salvador: Diocese of Santiago de Maria, 2008.
Guillen, Maria, ed. *Masacres: Trazos De La Historia Salvadorena Contados Por Las Victimas*. San Salvador, El Salvador: Centro de Derechos Humanos, 2006.
Gutierrez, Gustavo. *On Job: God-Talk and the Suffering of the Innocent*. New York: Orbis Books, 1987.
———. *A Theology of Liberation*. New York: Orbis Books, 1988.
———. *Las Casas: In Search of the Poor of Jesus Christ*. Translated by Robert R. Barr. Eugene, Oregon: Wipf and Stock Publishers, 1995.
Hernandez, Maria Julia. *Romero*. San Salvador, El Salvador: Asociacion Equipo Maiz, 2000.
Hovey, Craig. *To Share in the Body: A Theology of Martyrdom for Today's Church*. Grand Rapids, MI: Brazos Press, 2008.
Keogh, Dermot, ed. *Church and Politics in Latin America*. New York: St. Martin's Press, 1990.
Kiser, John W. *The Monks of Tibhirine: Faith, Love, and Terror in Algeria*. New York: St. Martin's Press, 2002.
Kelly, Thomas M. *When the Gospel Grows Feet: Rutilio Grande, SJ, and the Church in El Salvador; An Ecclesiology in Context*. Collegeville, Minnesota: Liturgical Press, 2013.
Le Breton, Binka. *The Greatest Gift: The Courageous Life and Martyrdom of Sister Dorothy Stang*. New York: Doubleday, 2007.

Leemans, Johan, ed. *More Than a Memory*. Leuven: Peeters, 2005.
Lopez Vigil, Maria. *Oscar Romero: Memories in Mosaic*. Translated by Kathy Ogle. Washington D.C.: EPICA, 2000.
Maier, Hans, ed. *Martyrium in 20. Jahrhundert*. Mooshausen: Ploger, 2004.
Maier, Martin. *Oscar Romero: Meister Der Spiritualität*. Freiburg, Germany: Herder, 2001.
———. "Monsenor Romero, Conflictividad Ecclesial Y Carino Ministerial." *Revista Latinoamericana de Teologia* 64, no. 22 (2005): 7–26.
———. *Monsenor Romero: Maestro De Espiritualidad*, Edited by UCA Editores. San Salvador, El Salvador: UCA Editores, 2005.
———. *Monsenor Romero: Maestro De Espiritualidad*. San Salvador, El Salvador: UCA Editores, 2005.
Martialay, Roberto SJ. *Sangre En La Universidad: Los Jesuitas Asesinados En El Salvador*. Bilbao, Spain: Ediciones Mensajero, 1999.
McBrien, Richard. *Catholicism*. New York: Harper Collins, 1994.
McGovern, Arthur F. *Liberation Theology and Its Critics: Toward an Assessment*. Maryknoll, NY: Orbis Books, 1989.
Metz, Johann Baptist. *Faith in History and Society: Toward a Practical Fundamental Theology*. New York: The Seaburg Press, 1980.
Metz, Johann Baptist and Schillebeeckx, Edward, ed. *Martyrdom Today*, Concilium. New York: The Seabury Press, 1983.
Montgomery, Tommie Sue. *Revolution in El Salvador: From Civil Strife to Civil Peace*. 2nd ed. San Francisco: Westview Press, 1995.
Moss, Candida. *Ancient Christian Martyrdom: Diverse Practices, Theologies and Traditions*. New Haven: Yale University Press, 2012.
Moss, Candida. *The Myth of Persecution: How Early Christians Invented a Story of Martyrdom*. New York: Harper One, 2013.
Muller, Greinacher and, ed. *The Poor and the Church*. New York: The Seabury Press, 1977.
Mulligan, Joseph E. SJ. *The Jesuit Martyrs of El Salvador: Celebrating the Anniversaries*. Baltimore, Maryland: Fortkamp Publishing Company, 1994.
Murphy, Roseanne. *Martyr of the Amazon: The Life of Sister Dorothy Stang*. New York: Orbis Books, 2007.
Nelson-Pallmeyer, Jack. *School of Assassins: Guns, Greed, and Globalization*. Maryknoll, New York: Orbis Books, 2001.
Noone, Judith M. *The Same Fate as the Poor*. New York: Maryknoll Sisters Publication, 1984.
O'Collins, Gerald. "The Resurrection of Jesus." In *Interpreting Jesus*. Ramsey, NJ: Paulist Press, 1983.
Okure, Sobrino, and Wilfred, ed. *Rethinking Martyrdom*, Concilium. London: SCM Press, 2003.
Peterson, Anna. *Martyrdom and the Politics of Religion*. Albany, NY: State University of New York Press, 1997.
Pope, Stephen, ed. *Hope and Solidarity: Jon Sobrino's Challenge to Christian Theology*. New York: Orbis Books, 2008.

Purcell, William. *Martyrs of Our Time*. St. Louis, MO: CBP Press, 1983.
Robert S. Pelton, CSC, ed. *Monsignor Romero: A Bishop for the Third Millenium*. Notre Dame, Indiana: University of Notre Dame Press, 2004.
Romero, Oscar A. *Archbishop Oscar Romero: A Shepherd's Diary*. Translated by Irene B. Hodgson. Cincinnati, Ohio: St. Anthony Messenger Press, 1993.
Romero, Oscar A. Romero. *Mons. Oscar A. Romero: Su Diaro*. San Salvador, El Salvador: Impreso de Talleres de Imprenta Criterio, 2000.
Royal, Robert. *The Catholic Martyrs of the Twentieth Century*. New York: The Crossroad Publishing Company, 2000.
Rufina Amaya, Mark Danner, and Carlos Henriquez. *Luciernagas En El Mozote*. San Salvador, El Salvador: Ediciones Museo de la Palabra, 1996.
Santiago, Daniel. *The Harvest of Justice: The Church of El Salvador Ten Years after Romero*. New York: Paulist Press, 1993.
Sittser, Gerard L. *Water from a Deep Well: Christian Spirituality from Early Martyrs to Modern Missionaries*. Downers Grove, IL: InterVarsity Press, 2007.
Sobrino, Jon. *Christology at the Crossroads: A Latin American Approach*. Translated by John Drury. New York: Orbis Books, 1978.
———. "El Martirio De Maura, Ita, Dorothy Y Jean." *Diakonia* 16, (1980): 2–6.
———. ed. *Companions of Jesus: The Jesuit Martyrs of El Salvador*. Maryknoll, New York: Orbis Books, 1990.
———. "El Seguimiento De Jesús Pobre Y Humilde. Como Bajar De La Cruz a Los Pueblos Crucificados." *Revista Latinoamericana de Teologia* 24, no. 8 (1991): 299–318.
———. *El Principio-Misericordia : Bajar De La Cruz a Los Pueblos Crucificados* Santander: Sal Terrae 1992.
———. "De Una Teología Sólo De La Liberación a Una Teología Del Martirio." *Revista Latinoamericana de Teologia* X, no. 28 (1993): 27–48.
———. *Jesus the Liberator: A Historical-Theological View*. Translated by Paul Burns and Francis McDonagh. Maryknoll, NY: Orbis Books, 1993.
———. *The Principle of Mercy : Taking the Crucified People from the Cross* Maryknoll, NY: Orbis Books, 1994.
———. *Monsenor Romero*. 3rd ed. San Salvador, El Salvador: UCA Editores 1995.
———. "Los Martires Jesuanicos Y El Pueblo Crucificado." *Paginas* XXV, no. 161 (2000): 45–61.
———. "Monseñor Romero: Cristiano Y Salvadoreño." *Revista Latinoamericana de Teología* XVII, no. 49 (2000): 25–36.
———. "Monseñor Romero: Exigencia, Juicio Y Buena Noticia. En El Xx Anniversario De Su Martirio." *Revista Latinoamericana de Teologia* XVII, no. 50 (2000): 191–207.
———. *Christ the Liberator: A View from the Victims*. Translated by Paul Burns. Maryknoll, NY: Orbis Books, 2001.
———. "La Utopia De Los Pobres Y El Reino De Dios." *Revista Latinoamericana de Teologia* 56, no. 19 (2002): 145–70.
———. "Nuestro Mundo, Crueldad Y Compasión." *Paginas*, no. 179 (2003): 44–52.

———. "Repensar El Martirio." *Revista internacional de Teologia Concilium* 299, no. 17 (2003): 173–205.

———. *Cartas a Ellacuría. 1989–2004.* Madrid: Editorial Trotta, 2004.

———. *Fuera De Los Pobres No Hay Salvacion.* Madrid: Editorial Trotta, 2007.

———. "Rutilio Grande: El Nacimiento De Una Iglesia Nueva, Salvadorena, Y Evangelica." *Revista Latinoamericana de Teologia* 70, (2007): 3–12.

———. "El Reino De Dios Y Jesús." *Concilium* 326, (2008): 399–409.

———. "Jesús De Galilea Desde El Contexto Salvadoreño. Compasión, Esperanza Y Seguimiento a La Luz De La Cruz." *Revista Latinoamericana de Teologia* XXV, no. 75 (2008): 313–34.

———. "Monseñor Romero: Conversión Y Esperanza." *Revista Latinoamericana de Teología* 80, (2010).

Sobrino, Jon and Ellacuria, Ignacio, ed. *Mysterium Liberationis: Fundamental Concepts of Liberation Theology.* New York Orbis Books, 1993.

Stalsett, Sturla J. *The Crucified and the Crucified: A Study in the Christology of Jon Sobrino.* Vol. 127 Studies in the Intercultural History of Christianity. Bern, Switzerland: Peter Lang, AG, 2003.

Tojeira, Jose Maria. *El Martirio Ayer Y Hoy.* San Salvador, El Salvador: UCA Editores 2005.

Urioste, Ricardo. *Evangelio Y Vida.* San Salvador, El Salvador: Equipo de Educacion Maiz, 1997.

Valiente, Orfilio Ernesto. "Truth, Justice, and Forgiveness: Reconciliation in Jon Sobrino's Christology" Dissertation, University of Notre Dame, 2010.

Whitfield, Teresa. *Paying the Price: Ignacio Ellacuria and the Murdered Jesuits of El Salvador.* Philadelphia: Temple University Press, 1995.

Index

action-reflection-action, 38
Allende, Salvador, 29
Anawim, 86
Ancient Christian Martyrdom (Moss), 4–5
Angelelli, Enrique, 28, 32n15
anonymous martyrs: argument for, 104; cases of, 13; from El Mozote massacre, 55; as forgotten, 50, 106; naming, 100; proposal of, 22n16; reality of, 18, 21; remembering, 108–109; significance of, 56; with small m, 105; suggestions of, x; types of, 108; of UCA community, 108
Anselmian theory, 74, 90
Aquinas, Thomas, 5, 10, 13, 14
Argentina, 27–28
Augustine, Saint, 5, 14, 43

Barrera, Facundo, 36
beatification: cause for Grande, 42; of Romero, x–xi, 11, 93, 104, 107
Beckett, Thomas, 17
Bernal, Mario, 40, 58n32
Berryman, Phillip, 35
Boff, Leonardo, ix, 5, 14
Bolivia, 86
Bonhoeffer, Dietrich, 74, 96
Brazil, 27–28, 56

A Brief History of Saints (Cunningham), 1
Buckland, Eric, 53–54
Burke, Kevin, 21, 109

Calvin, John, 6
Câmara, Helder, 27
campesinos, 38–39, 45, 47–48, 51, 57n16
Campion, Edmund, 5, 7n18
canonization, 15, 46, 61, 99, 104, 107. *See also* beatification; saints
Cardenal, Rodolfo, 45, 54
Carter, Jimmy, 48, 51
Casaldaliga, Pedro, 46
Catholic Action, 26–27, 28
Catholic Social Action, 28–29
CEBs. *See* Christian base communities
CELAM. *See* Latin American Bishops Conference
Chávez, Luis, 36, 39–40, 44
Chile, 28–30, 86
Christian base communities (CEBs), 27, 29–30, 37, 48
Christianity: early, as subversive, 14; missionaries of, 6; movement to Greco-Roman world, 97; persecution and, 3; as religion, 5; roots of, 1
Christology: good works and, 97; Latin American, 71, 85; liberation, 71;

117

new, 44, 84; of Sobrino, xi, 30, 44, 67–79, 83, 93, 104
Christology at the Crossroads (Sobrino): cross in, 71–73; discipleship in, 75–76; kingdom of God in, 76–79; review of, 67–79; theology in, 70
Christ the Liberator (Sobrino): cross in, 86–89; ideals developed in, 74; insights from, x; kingdom of God in, 86–89; martyrdom in, 83–100; reality in, 97–100; release of, 84; resurrection in, 95–97; scandal of cross in, 90–91; victims and violence in, 89
Church of Two Christendoms, 27
Clarke, Maura: as churchwoman in El Salvador, 48–51; as Jesuanic martyr, 51, 54; as Maryknoll missionary, 49; murder of, 30, 50, 63n83, 63n86; working with poor, 96
Claver, Saint Peter, 26
Clement of Rome, 3
Committee of Co-Operation for Peace (COPACHI), 29, 33n23
Companions of Jesus: The Jesuit Martyrs of El Salvador (Sobrino), 54
Constantine: Edict of Toleration, 2; martyrdom after, 5–6
conversion, 6, 19, 44, 48, 78, 85, 95
COPACHI. *See* Committee of Co-Operation for Peace
Cortina, Jon, 54, 65n105
Council of Chalcedon, 70–71
Cristeros movement, 22n1, 26–27
Cristiani, Alfredo, 52–54
Cristología desde Latinoamérica (Sobrino), 39
cross: in *Christology at the Crossroads*, 71–73; in *Christ the Liberator*, 86–89; crucified peoples and, 96; humanity of Jesus and, 74; in *Jesus the Liberator*, 86–89; in Latin America, 73; martyrdom and, 105; mystery of, 91; relationship to martyrdom, 73–75; as sacrifice, 98; scandal of, 90–91; united with resurrection, 99
crucified peoples: cross and, 96; Ellacuría coining, 17, 68, 85, 87, 94, 100n6, 101n26; expanding martyrdom, 18, 100; focus on, x; grace for, 99; in *Jesus the Liberator*, 91–94; Latin America and, 91; plight of, 95; poor and, 19; reality and, 20; Sobrino on, x, 16, 18, 21, 72, 84, 87
The Crucified God (Moltmann), 53, 92
Crusades, 1, 22n13
Cunningham, Larry, 2–4, 9–11, 14, 108

Dear, John, 44
death threats: to Grande, 40; to Romero, 46–47; to sisters, 49; to UCA community, 47
Delgado, Jesus, 43, 46–47
Delp, Alfred, 96
Deposito Martyrum, 3
Dirty War, 28
disappeared, 11, 26–30, 32n5
discipleship, 75–76, 85
docetism, 19–20, 75, 98
Dominicans, 6
Donovan, Jean: bill sent to family of, 63n87; as churchwoman of El Salvador, 48; as Jesuanic martyr, 51, 54; as Maryknoll missionary, 49; murder of, 30, 50, 63n83, 63n86; working with poor, 96
Duarte, José Napoleón, 55

Easter Sunday, 73, 86–87
Edict of Toleration, 2
Ellacuría, Ignacio: on burden of reality, 23n58; crucified people coined by, 17, 68, 85, 87, 94, 100n6, 101n26; as Jesuanic martyr, 20; murder of, 16, 53–54; on poor, 85; return of, 96; search for, 52; on side of poor, 97; supporting Romero, 45; as target, 64n95; theology of, 44; as witness, 99

El Salvador: Civil War, xi, 30–31; death squads of, 10; El Mozote massacre, 55; reality in, 56, 70, 84; research in, ix–x; U.S. churchwomen in, 48–51, 63n83
Espinoza, Lt., 52, 64n96
Estrada, Benito, 59n35

Faith in History in Society (Metz), 67
Falange, 58n28
Farabundo Martí National Liberation Front (FMLN), 51, 53, 55, 65n101, 65n105
Felicity, Saint, 2
Fe y Alegría Schools, 26, 31n4, 52
flogged Christs, 84
FMLN. *See* Farabundo Martí National Liberation Front
Ford, Ita: as churchwoman in El Salvador, 48–51; as Jesuanic martyr, 51; as Maryknoll missionary, 49; murder of, 30, 50, 63n83, 63n86; working with poor, 96

Francis, Pope: call on martyrdom, x–xi, 101n42, 103–107, 110n1; on marginalized, 106
Franciscans, 6
Francis of Assisi, 18

Gandhi, Mohandas, 109
Gerardi, Juan José, 56, 99, 108
gladiators, 9
gnosticism, 98
Gonzalez, San Roque, 7n19
Good Friday, 73, 86
good works, 97
Gospel: action-reflection-action in, 38; becoming, 3; Christ in, 86; identifying with, 28; of John, 76, 87; message, 14, 42; truths, 11
Grande, Rutilio: advocacy of, 39; ambush and assassination of, 41, 67; birth and early life, 35–36; branded communist priest, 38, 57n15; cause for beatification, 42; death threats to, 40; homilies of, 39–40, 58n25, 58n32, 86; as Jesuanic martyr, 54, 94; martyrdom, 30–31, 56; ministering by, 38; ordination of, 36; pastoral action plan of, 36–39; preaching by, 39–41, 58n32, 86, 106; reminding of injustice, 109; Romero influenced by, 44–45; Romero on, 41–42; seminary study and professorship, 36; statements about, 104; as target of paramilitary groups, 35
Guatemala, 30, 56
gulags, ix, 9, 10
Gutiérrez, Gustavo, 27, 46

Hogar de Cristo, 26, 31n4
Holy Innocents, 5, 17
homilies: of Grande, 39–40, 58n25, 58n32, 86; of Romero, 30, 41–42, 45–47, 60n54, 61n67, 61n70
Hurtado, Alberto, 26, 31n4

Ignatius of Antioch, 3
Imitation of Christ (Thomas a Kempis), 43
Institute for Latin American Pastoral Work, 37
Islam, ix, 1, 9

Jesuanic martyrs: Clarke as, 51, 54; defined, 11; Donovan as, 51, 54; Ellacuría as, 20; expanding martyrdom, 67, 100; Ford as, 51, 54; Grande as, 54, 94; Kazel as, 51, 54; Romero as, 42, 54, 94, 96; Sobrino coining, x, 11, 17, 19–20, 53, 65n109, 79, 83, 94–95, 104, 106; from UCA community, 51–54, 83–84, 92, 94–95
Jesuits: ; reductions, 6, 7n19, 26; threats against, 35; *See also* UCA community
Jesus Christ: early life of, 2; in Gospel, 86; historical view of, 71; humanity

of, 74, 84; Jesus martyrs, 11, 16–18, 20–21; liberation and, 77; memory of, 21; preaching of, 14–15, 77; as proto-martyr, 2–5, 88, 94, 98; resurrection of, 21, 26, 73, 76, 85, 89; Sobrino on following of, 19–20; Suffering Servant of Yahweh, 18, 84–85, 96

Jesus the Liberator (Sobrino): cross in, 86–89; crucified people in, 91–94; insights from, x; kingdom of God in, 86–89; martyrdom in, 83–100; reality in, 97–100; release of, 83–84; resurrection in, 95–97; scandal of cross in, 90–91; victims and violence in, 89

John of the Cross, 43
John Paul II, xi, 10–11, 28, 53
José Ramirez, Juan, 40
justice, martyrs for, x, 93, 100, 104, 107, 108
Justin Martyr, 1

Kasper, Walter, 19
Kazel, Dorothy: as churchwoman in El Salvador, 48–51; as Jesuanic martyr, 51, 54; murder of, 30, 50, 63n86; as Ursuline missionary, 49; working with poor, 96
Kelly, Thomas M., 36, 39
King, Martin Luther, 20, 94
kingdom of God, 76–79, 86–89, 99
Kolbe, Maximillian, 13
Kolvenbach, Peter Hans, 53

Las Casas, Bartolomé de, 25–26
Last Supper, 88
Latin America: Argentina, 27–28; Brazil, 27–28, 56; Chile, 28–30, 86; Christology, 71, 85; cross in, 73; crucified people and, 91; martyrdom, 25–31; political deaths in, 9, 32n5; poor, 96; reality of 20th and 21st centuries, 25–27, 55, 85, 89; theologians, 71; Vatican II and,

69–70; violence in, 16–17; *See also* El Salvador; *specific countries*
Latin American Bishops Conference (CELAM), 36, 109
Laudato Si (Francis), 106
Lemus, Nelson Rutilio, 41
Leo XIII, 38
Letter of the Martyrdom of Polycarp, 3
liberation: ; Christology, 71; Jesus Christ and, 77; *See also Christ the Liberator* (Sobrino); *Jesus the Liberator* (Sobrino)
Lopez, Amando, 53
Lopez, Efraim, 49
López y López, Joaquín, 52–53, 65n100
Lumen Gentium, 70
Luther, Martin, 6

Maccabees, 1, 6
Maier, Martin, 42–44
Martin-Baró, Ignacio, 53, 64n97
martyrdom: broadening concept of, 10–11, 14, 67, 108–109; call from Pope Francis, x–xi, 101n42, 103–107, 110n1; in *Christ the Liberator*, 83–100; cross and, 73–75, 105; crucified peoples expanding, 18, 100; defined, 93; of Grande, 30–31, 56; history of, x; in *Jesus the Liberator*, 83–100; Latin America, 25–31; Rahner on broadening, 14, 83; reality of, 103–110; of Romero, 56; Sobrino development of, 73–75, 83–100; Sobrino on, 103–107; three-tiered expansion of, 108–109
martyrdom, contemporary: overview, 9–11; rethinking, 15–21; in today's world, 12–15
martyrdom, defining: after Constantine, 5–6; overview, 1; search for definition, 1–2
The Martyrdom of Polycarp, 2, 5
Martyrdom Today (Metz and Schillebeeckx), 12
martyred people, x, 92–94, 100

Martyria, 3
Martyrium, 2
martyrs: with capital M, 105–106, 108–109; cult of, 4; defined, 93; derivation of term, 2; Jesus Christ as proto-martyr, 2–5; Jesus martyrs, 11, 16–18, 20–21; for justice, x, 93, 100, 104, 107, 108; Polycarp as proto-martyr, 2–5; of poor, 105; prophetic stance of, 11; red, 109; relics of, 5; Sobrino and, 78; of UCA community, 51–54, 83–84, 92, 94–95; veneration of, 4–5; *See also* anonymous martyrs; crucified peoples; Jesuanic martyrs
Marxism, 37, 60n52
metanoia, 15, 19
Metz, Johann Baptist, ix, 12, 21, 67
Mexico: church and government in, 26; *Cristeros* movement, 26–27
Mignon, Emilio, 28
mission of compassion, 20
The Mission, 6
Molina, Arturo, 30, 58n27
Moltmann, Jurgen, 53, 69, 72–73
Montes, Segundo, 52–53, 64n96
More, Thomas, 5
Moreno, Juan Ramón, 53–54, 92
Moss, Candida, 4
El Mozote massacre, 55, 109
Mulligan, Joe, 52
Murphy, John, 58n31

Navarro, Alfonso, 45, 60n57
Nicaragua, 30

odium fidei, 17, 56, 93, 103, 106, 108
otherness, 98

Palacios, Rafael, 40
panegyrics, 59n46
Pannenberg, Wolfhart, 69
paramilitary groups, 35
Passio, 2
Passionist priests, 44, 60n53

The Passion of Perpetual and Felicity, 2
pastoral action plan, 36–39
Paul VI, 37–38, 41
Perpetua, Saint, 2
Peter, Saint, 5
Peterson, Anna, 35
Pinochet, Augusto, 28–30
Pius X, 38
Pohl, Mauricio Borgonovo, 45, 60n57
political holiness, 14–15
political love, 15
Polycarp, Saint: as author, 1; commemoration of, 2; Letter of the Martyrdom of Polycarp, 3; as proto-martyr, 2–5
poor: Clarke working with, 96; crucified peoples and, 19; Donovan working with, 96; Ellacuría on, 85; Ellacuría on side of, 97; Ford working with, 96; Kazel working with, 96; kingdom of God and, 99; Latin America, 96; martyrs of, 105; Romero on side of, 17–18, 20, 46, 86, 97–98
Popieluszko, Jerzy, 11
Populorum Progressio (Paul VI), 37–38
preaching: by Grande, 39–41, 58n32, 86, 106; of Jesus Christ, 14–15, 77; practice and, 77; of Romero, 31, 45–46, 96, 107; on social justice, 62
Pro, Miguel, 9, 22n1, 26–27
prophetic stance, 11

Rahner, Karl: on action, 12; on broadening martyrdom, 14, 83, 108; challenge of, 10–11; complicated cases and, 13; discussion of, 5; influencing Sobrino, 69; on intention, 12–13; theology of, ix
Ramos, Celina, 52–54, 64n99, 99, 109
Ramos, Elba, 52–54, 64n99, 109
Reagan, Ronald, 35, 48
reality: of anonymous martyrs, 18, 21; in *Christ the Liberator*, 97–100; crucified peoples and, 20; Ellacuría on burden of, 23n58; in El Salvador,

56, 70, 84; in *Jesus the Liberator*, 97–100; Latin America of 20th and 21st centuries, 25–27, 55, 85, 89; of martyrdom, 103–110; Sobrino on, 20–21, 30
red martyrs, 109
reformation, 1, 5
relics, 5
resurrection: cross united with, 99; of Jesus Christ, 21, 26, 73, 76, 85, 89; Sobrino on, 21, 95–97
Rethinking Martyrdom, 15–21
Romans, ix, 1–2, 4, 9, 14, 77
Romero, Oscar: as archbishop, 31, 44–47; assassination of, 30, 47, 61n70; beatification of, x–xi, 11, 93, 104, 107; birth and early life of, 42–43; complicated case of, 13; death of, x; death threats to, 46–47; descriptions of, 17; Ellacuría supporting, 45; on Grande, 41–42; Grande's influence on, 44–45; homilies and writings of, 30, 41–42, 45–47, 60n54, 61n67, 61n70; impact of, 45; as Jesuanic martyr, 42, 54, 94, 96; letter to Sobrino, 46; martyrdom, 56; Nobel Prize nomination, 45; panegyrics and, 59n46; parish of, 43; political holiness and, 15; preaching of, 31, 45–46, 96, 107; real church of, 98; reminding of injustice, 109; on side of poor, 17–18, 20, 46, 86, 97–98; Sobrino on death of, 48; study and ordination, 43; tomb of, ix–x, 11; as witness, 99
Royal, Robert, 26–27

saints: with capital S and with small s, 105; political, 15; reverence of, 109; Sobrino on, 18; veneration of, 5
salvation, 74, 88, 90–91, 98, 106, 110
Schillebeeckx, Edward, 12
Servil, Bernardo, 40
Silva Henríquez, Raúl, 29
sin, 77–78, 90
Smith, Brian, 29
Sobrino, Jon: Christology of, xi, 30, 44, 67–79, 83, 93, 104; on Christ's death, 92; cross and, 71–73; on crucified peoples, x, 16, 18, 21, 72, 84, 87; discipleship and, 75–76, 85; editing of, 15–21; on Eucharistic Procession, 45–46; on following of Jesus, 19–20; insights of, x; intellectual biography of, 68–70; Jesuanic martyr coined by, x, 11, 17, 19–20, 53, 65n109, 79, 83, 94–95, 104, 106; kingdom of God and, 76–79, 86–89; on martyrdom, 103–107; martyrdom development and, 73–75, 83–100; martyrs and, 78; on mission of compassion, 20; murder in room of, 53; political holiness and, 14–15; Rahner influencing, 69; on reality, 20–21, 30; on resurrection, 21, 95–97; Romero letter to, 46; on Romero's death, 48; on saints, 18; on salvation, 91; on sin, 77–78; on surrender, 78; theological training of, 68–69; on UCA community murders, 54; on U.S. churchwomen, 50–51; on violent deaths, 16–18, 89
Solórzano, Manuel, 41
Southwell, Robert, 5, 7n18
Stang, Dorothy, 28, 56, 108
Stein, Edith, 10
Stephen, Saint, 1
Suffering Servant of Yahweh, 18, 84–85, 96
surrender, 78

Un Techo para Chile, 26, 31n4
Tejada, Vicente, 35–36
Teresa of Ávila, 43
theodicy, 72, 90, 96
Thomas a Kempis, 43
Tiburine monks, ix
Tojeira, José María, 53
Tortolo, Adolfo, 28

UCA community: anonymous martyrs of, 108; death threats to, 47; Jesuanic martyrs of, 51–54, 83–84, 92, 94–95; killings at, x, 16; Sobrino on murders in, 54; 25th anniversary of, 109; workers, 45
United Nations Truth Commission, 35
Urioste, Ricardo, 44, 47, 62n71
U.S. churchwomen: in El Salvador, 48–51; murder of, 50, 63n83, 67; reminding of injustice, 109; Sobrino on, 50–51; *See also* Clarke, Maura; Donovan, Jean; Ford, Ita; Kazel, Dorothy
Ut Unum Sint (John Paul II), 10–11

Valiente, Ernesto, 68, 69
Vatican II, 17, 36, 69–70, 103, 105
Vicaría de la Solidaridad, 29

will of God, 3, 19

Zwingli, Hyldrych, 6

About the Author

John Thiede, SJ is an Assistant Professor of Theology at Marquette University in Milwaukee, Wisconsin, specializing in Christology and Latin American Theology. He has published articles on Sister Dorothy Stang and the Good of Creation and on *Laudato Si'* from a liberation theology perspective. Originally from Plymouth, Minnesota he is a priest of the Wisconsin Province of the Society of Jesus.

www.ingramcontent.com/pod-product-compliance
Ingram Content Group UK Ltd.
Pitfield, Milton Keynes, MK11 3LW, UK
UKHW021310180426
11947UKWH00015B/1147